orange

pussy

small
hands

she
deserves
it

leaks

too
long to
Pee

Lies

$

Stormy

dump

fake
news

fucked
up

sad

extremely
careless

$

Resist

hole

a
blow
out

hair
hair

pantsuit

dick
pic

deleted
email

wiener
weiner

grateful

GRABBING PUSSY

GRABBING PUSSY

KAREN FINLEY

OR Books

New York • London

All rights information: rights@orbooks.com
Visit our website at www.orbooks.com

First printing 2018.

Library of Congress Cataloging-in-Publication Data: A catalog record for this book is available from the Library of Congress.

British Library Cataloging in Publication Data: A catalog record for this book is available from the British Library.

Design and typesetting by Elyse J. Strongin, Neuwirth & Associates.
Illustrations by Karen Finley.

Published for the book trade by OR Books in partnership with Counterpoint Press.
Distributed to the trade by Publishers Group West.

paperback ISBN 978-1-944869-95-3
ebook ISBN 978-1-944869-96-0

For Pony

FUCK POLITICS

"And he [Rubio] referred to my hands, 'if they're small something else must be small.' I guarantee you there's no problem, I guarantee it."

Look at my hands
Measure them to yours
They aren't small hands.
Are they?
I do wonder. Let me move them in front of you quickly
With my crack, a rant attack of alternative facts
Losing meaning to the facts
This hand has built and squeezed every last cent, any cents,
     any sense of you
This hand is a small hand
It is large enough, this hand
Fuck politics and everything about it
I want to fuck the politics out of you
I want to fuck the politics into you
Pussy prick
Please Putin
Where are we in all of this genital election?

Of pussy grabbing the lack of penis backpack
The ability to *men u strate*
Takes–over–the–consciousness–of–everything–else state.

I will fuck politics from behind and then turn her over
Till she squeals for more
Till they tell me how they like it
Let me fuck
Till it hurts me more than you
Fuck Politics

PUSSY POWER

"I'm automatically attracted to beautiful [women]—I just start kissing them. It's like a magnet. Just kiss. I don't even wait. And when you're a star they let you do it. You can do anything . . ."

When I You We wait on the bus not like Rosa Parks
But like a slobbering school idiot maniac white middle-
    aged rich triumphant ego sniveling surveying asshole
    that never took a bus anywhere
Your ability
When you use *you*
When you *is* you

    My time is spent grabbing pussy like I really want to really
    grab your dick. What I do is when I am threatened by
    male desire—I man up. *Let me man up.* It is in these poetics
    of allowed franchised spaces of men connecting like a circle
    jerk my hands move as I talk in circle jerk formations,
    twisting with the rhythm of my pee on the snow, my
    cream whizz on the breeze – but I am on the bus and the
    memory won't take hold of me. Billy Bush is sitting close
    and his legs and breath are hovering near. I can feel the
    sensation of his voice brush against my neck. *Let me man
    up.* Let me take a breath and resist the urge to undo the
    long red tie that shields my crotch. I can feel the pressure

build, of his leg near mine. *Let me man up.* The tension escalates so I better speak of pussy, of conquests inside the bus like speaking of like a circle jerk. *Let me man up.* Let me take the lead in watching women so I don't watch your male pumped body and you don't see my quavering frame. *Let me man up.*

Where I sublimate my own curiosity, my desire for you.

To grab you

Grab some dick

Grab some penis

Boys grab it

Girls grab it

I better not

Let me grab me some pussy

Bite off man's naughty bits

And feel my small manhood, my small hands

Like a slender dove that creates

Sign language to interpret

In the air

Fly away coo coo

As my hair swept back

A macaw

A bird a fowl

Pussy might find me

For her supper

In private I will let you call me

Kitty

Meow

GRABBING PUSSY

"Grab them by the pussy. You can do anything."

Grabbing pussy has always been hard (no pun intended)
Grabbing pussy is a challenge even for those who live
    in one
To hold onto labia—to get your pinky hooked on clitoris
To let your claws hold onto the mane
Pray tell or prey tell pussy tell me please let me hang on
    your grace
Grabbing pussy has the consequences of digging deep into
    the interior
Clutching canal of wetness
The folding petals of wonderment that enclose onto the
    unseen
Grab them by the pussy
Grab her like a bitch.

Let me grab pussy, physically hold onto pussy to
    psychically navigate
With all my physical presence has to offer grabbing the soft
    tissue surrounding the entrance of desire
I won't be invited and need to force myself in
My own primal scream my memory birth
Let me grab pussy

Grabbing childlike hands, fingers into cookie jars

Cold pizza go grab a slice

A steak well done with ketchup

Grabber Grabber Grab her

My pussy is a cup of coffee in this cold morning
    without you.

Grab me some pussy

That angry cat

Make her purr—lion roar

A pussy

I'm one angry cat

Vulva victoriouslicous

Very vulva very veryberry vulva

She said he's a pussy

I'm the pussy

Call me a shiver quiver

Cunt angry

Vagjaglagragtagbaggaghagnagsagbragflagdrag anything
    or they will think I'm a fag

Oh, Pussy, I need you so, for without you I have nothing
    to fear and destroy

Nothing to navigate my withered self

Help me, Pussy

Be a good Puss
And help me grow
To expand my vocabulary
Words, image
Here you go

My ABCs
Apple Pie Abalone Angel Fish
Box Bottom Bravo
Conch shell Coobie Cubby hole Cooch Cha-cha
Delight Dog house Danger Ditch Dove
Electric Eel Elevator shaft
Fresh Fish Folded Fins
Glorious Garage Gallivanter Goo
Hamburger Helper Heaven Handle
Ice cream soft serve time
Jamming Jelly Jewelry box
Kangaroo pouch Kitchen mitt mixer
Lamb Lick Locket
Momma I'm home Milk and honey
Nookie Nancy best Nest
Oh my god Oh my goddess
Pen holder
Queen bee hive

River she keeps

Squeezebox

Taco mouth

Undercover beaver snapper

Volvo lips

Wet Whore nurse

XXX

Y? because it feels good

Zzzzz time to sleep after I lose myself in you

Megyn Kelly: "You've called women you don't like 'fat pigs,' 'dogs,' 'slobs' and 'disgusting animals.' . . . You once told a contestant on 'Celebrity Apprentice' it would be a pretty picture to see her on her knees. Does that sound to you like the temperament of a man we should elect as president . . .?"

Donald Trump: "She gets out and she starts asking me all sorts of ridiculous questions. You could see there was blood coming out of her eyes, blood coming out of her wherever."

It's a war on women
A bimbo
A bleeding woman
A menstruating woman
Period.
A Medea a Medusa a Megyn
A megGYN a gynecological exam
An over-grown over-groin emotional
Where-ever where-wolf whore-wolf
Here-wolf
Are you on the rag?
Are you on the rag?
Your hysteria
To go find, identify, and accuse

A bleeding woman grabby grab me grubby pussy
The humiliation
To reduce to
Bleeding from wherever
Bleeding from wherever
Bleeding from wherever
Bleeding from wherever
The image of the bleeding woman
Her stains and drips
Her signed sealed and delivered
Her cramps belts pads and cotton
Her applicators and residue
Her egg released from you
Bleeding from wherever
Living with your wet dream of misogyny
Sent to the blood shut hut
By the blood hound found
For you don't shut up
Shut the fuck up
I said SHUT THE FUCK UP

The potential to be mother to create life
The hostility from the fear of "on the rag"
Is it disgusting?

From prayer and sanctity

To isolate evacuate intimidate

We have been shown the bleeding woman in politics
    before

Jackie standing next to LBJ

Taking oath was on the rag

Blood smeared pink suit

Brain stain

Or the red hole

The Red Whole

Don't ever send me red roses

The red maroon the flame fire hates

Blood coming out of her eyes

Your splendid coiffed magnificence startles his own blonde
    inadequacy

And the Donald sees red

Your ability to call on him in front of everyone

Trump would remind Medusa that she would soon be
    raped by Poseidon

And he was afraid that her stare could reduce him to stone

Her potency begins when he attacked her

Rather than an apology

Cathartic entertainment ploy

Of parting the red sea formed by Medusa Megyn's blood
Sprinkled onto seaweed
Woman's heart is her head a snake a phallus is her
    empowered brain
The anger to demand of the woman
He objects insults ridicules
Desires degrades despairs
For the bleeding woman, a misplaced loathing
As he never is able to wash away his own distress
His own castrating fear
The wounded gash to claim his own
His red tie tide
Scream
Scream
What didn't you receive
How bad
How crazy
Seeing red
SAD!

Call her a dog
A cunt
A bitch
A cow

Call her a pussy

A meow

Call her a dog in heat

A pig

Call her ugly, Big Ugly, Real Ugly

A monkey

An ape

Call her a snake

A bitch a butch

A whore

Call her anything or not at all

Call her anything you want

She's a bleeding injured creature

A piece of meat

Roadkill

Call her a jackass, donkey, a horse, a mule

Tiger

Cunt

Wench

Ho

Reduce it to a sense, a smell

Stank and stench

Fish fry

Bring on the mud, the dirt

With hog, oink and moo
A queef
Or her overall arching trying to fit in with some broken-
 down ideal of beauty
From Ivana to Ivanka to Marla to Tiffany to Melania to
Megyn
Bring on the teeth and nails
A dyke a slut on good days
An attractive derogatory wagger prick pleaser
Who puts out

All girl
A femme who is as far away from Mars
As possible

Blonde art part of the deal
Isn't Trump the Bimbo?
Oh, dear you are!
You have been hiding for dear life
And now we see you
In all your voluptuous glory
And heavy makeup and dyed teased hair

For bimbo is Italian for male baby

Hello male baby

A female is a bimba

You dim wit bimbo Dumpf

Why haven't we seen you?

Here I am everyone, your bimbo, *who you hate*

I present myself as promiscuous and on the prowl

But not necessarily the smartest growl

I am the blonde joke

I am your bleeding heart busty bimbo

Marry me.

ROSIE O'DONNELL

During the first Republican primary debate in August 2015, Fox News host Megyn Kelly asked Trump about past comments he made about women, calling them "fat pigs, dogs, slobs and disgusting animals."

"Only Rosie O'Donnell," Trump quipped.

At the September 27, 2016 debate, he said, "Somebody who has been very vicious to me, Rosie O'Donnell, I said very tough things to her and I think everybody would agree that she deserves it and nobody feels sorry for her."

Trump tweets:

> "I feel sorry for Rosie 's new partner in love whose parents are devastated at the thought of their daughter being with @Rosie-- a true loser."
>
> "Rosie is crude, rude, obnoxious and dumb—other than that I like her very much!"

How can one person—one woman—bring about such venom?

Trump speak: When you spot it, you got it. I have children, wives, buildings, status. I have deals, bankruptcies, finance. Yet, I don't have what Rosie has . . .

Rosie allows her body to be her body that I can attack, that I can verbally abuse and control. I look at Rosie and I am able to project onto her what I try to demean in myself. It would be suspect if I attacked a male gay celebrity—it would threaten publicly my own hidden shame of my vulnerable masculinity.

I cannot stand next to Rosie for Rosie will not shut up. Rosie will not project an image of desire to sustain the image of the man I need to project. Rosie will not answer to me. Rosie has her own clout, her own money, her own ratings.

Rosie does not have the right stuff for feminine-dominant femme portrayals and that runs deep with me and my insecurities. Rosie does not grant me the space to be able to assert my male influence. Rosie laughs at me. She is able to get others to laugh at me.

SAD.

Rosie is a place where I can put down her character, attributes that I am trying to keep down in myself. Figure it out.

But Rosie also mocked and got too close, she got way too close, making fun of my hair, my fetish, drag accessory, my merkin, my teased bouffant. I am Divine in *Female Trouble*. These are my safe spaces for communicating my gender, my repressed fluidity, my gender expression that I both hate and desire simultaneously.

That was the big no-no.
Do not make fun of Mommy's hair I mean Donald's hair—

My hair do, my hair don't. My dippity do don't
Won't go away
Plenty of spray
Straightened, shagged
Feathered, ready to fly
I'm Farrah
Charlie's Angels doll
With plenty of volume
Easy, sassy
Both sporty and dressy
I'm that kind of ready
Tapered into a wedge
A blow away
A blow dry but I prefer it
The Donald way
A *blow out*
Extend straight out from
A peaking forehead
Asymmetrical
Beehive
Bettie Page

Give me Big Hair

Blow ME out

No blunt cut

No bob cut

Yes, to bouffant

Brush cut

Jones-ing for a man bun

Or pig tails down my back

I'm a 10

No buzzed or crew

At home, I keep my hair for a chignon

With a comb-over

A curtain side part

It's a devil lock

A duck ass

A long fade

A fingered dick wave

Flipped

I would love a French twist

Give me frosted tips

A full crown clown

Extensions

Or half crown

Half up
Half down
Highlights layers too
Liberty spikes
Long hair
A mod cut
Freakish manic mullet
Page boy
A strong part
Pompadour, love a pony hawk
A psycho-Billy wedge
A whiff, a rat tail, a shingle bob
Slicked back, surfer, tail on top
Up do wings
Call me crazy, call me nuts
Just call me a candidate with
a *blow out.*

Rosie has everything I want and can't have
I project onto Rosie because I can
She made it on her own.
She is out—her desire, her love, her relationship.
She has humor. I don't have humor.

Have you ever seen me laugh?

Her presence of not desiring me—her presentation
    not in place to influence or be in relationship to my
    masculinity, as feminine submissive.

She dominates, threatens the wall I have built to insulate
    and hide my own attraction.

I'm the pig, the disgusting pig.

I'm the bitch.

The slobbering idiot.

The real loser.

Rosie is a real loser, a woman out of control

I am a real loser, a woman out of control

You can't make false statements

I can make false statements

My nice fat little Rosie

My nice little fat Donny

I feel sorry for Rosie's partner

I feel sorry for my partner

Only Rosie. I only said this about Rosie.

Fat pig, dogs, slobs, disgusting animals.

Only Rosie Only Rosie O'Donnell

Rosie O'Donnell

It was the teasing

My inner Rosie

My inner drama drag princess

Rosie

Rosy Oh Donald

Rosie oh Donnelled

My inner drama drag princess

The hive of my face my blush my rose

My rosy tight asshole

My head of state my blush of being found out

Rosy OH DonalD

Mother cried oh Rosy lass, alas lad

That was to be my name

Oh, Briar Rosy

Thorns and all

Rosy Oh Donald

My drag name

A queen for a day

The slob

The pig

The loser

Mommy I'm a winner–this fat pig, dog, slob, disgusting
  animal
This Rosy Oh Donald is a winner.

TRUMP FUCKED UP

"Look at those hands, are they small hands?" the front-runner for the GOP presidential nomination said, raising them for viewers to see. "And, he referred to my hands—'if they're small, something else must be small.' I guarantee you there's no problem. I guarantee."

Dear Mr. Trump,

We are so happy to know and greatly relieved to know that your penis is guaranteed to be working just fine. We as a nation are rest assured by the working order, size, construction, demolition, and planning of your penis. As a man who likes to build things, the comparison is clear. We really don't care, but we are rest assured that you took the time, your valuable time away from important matters of the economy, the state, and the well-being of our citizens to spend time on this important matter of your penis size. We are so relieved that you straightened it out. Since the beginning of time we have known about the fear of men and the size of their instrument and you have let us be aware that this is what drives you—the size and working order of your penis. Of course, it is an imperative and personal matter of the body—but is it that it might not always work? Just wondering.

Since we know from your Twitter feed and rallies and golf games that you don't get out much, and that you don't read

or explore or reflect, that you're not curious—we wanted
to let you know that *it* doesn't always work, and with age
and experience and sometimes by design or one's own state
of emotions or being aroused, we as a nation of millions
have varying degrees of experiences of a working penis, and
truthfully, we all have arrived here in one form or another
because of the working penis. The penis does not make the man
or the woman. It is the person who makes the penis. You could
be a bit more creative and less provincial about your ideas of the
penis. Please be more open about your gender fluidity, Donald!

We understand from the history of ruthless dictators the
concern with the size, virility, potency, and masculinity that
has driven them to conquer, and you let us know with your
generous anecdotes that you are in this particular category.
You are concerned with the amount, the polls, the finish line,
the winning—and everyone else is a big failure, or a loser.
Your continued performance of exaggerating non-existent
accomplishments are *sad* attempts to prop up your own
pathetic big dick promotion. And as your constituency we
mock you jubilantly as our fool president. Fools happen.

We as a nation are assured when you tell us this vital
information, that your penis is *just fine*. We were so worried.
We were so concerned! It was such an issue for us as voters!

We stopped thinking about the terrorism, war, poverty, suffering, taxes, poisoned water, police brutality, and instead we were thinking about whether your masculinity could stand to attention! We had your penis on our minds and quite frankly on our lips. We do hope that you feel the rush of everyone being aware of your potency. Not since Tricky Dick have we all *come together* with a penis quandary, but since you have such a strong record of telling the truth we will believe you that your penis is just fine and in working order.

Would it be possible for you to describe your working penis in more detail? It would be wonderful since you won't show your taxes, instead you could show your penis or your balls. You could arrange a leak? Just asking.

But might we mention that the penis doesn't have to do anything or accomplish anything to be a penis? Like the crowd size at your inauguration—it does seem to be a displaced concern for another size issue that you can't come to terms with. Your concern about the size of the crowd–was bigger than Obama's? We all saw it—you had a smaller much smaller crowd. So we get it. You have a smaller penis and that is your problem. And now that is our problem. *Size matters.*

Thanks,

Your Supporters

PS. Just wanting to give a suggestion here: After the recording of you saying "grab 'em by the pussy," many of your supporters wanted to *see* you say the word *pussy* rather than just hear it. We wonder if your mouth would pucker like a rosebud, or if we would see some tongue. You have such a sweet small mouth that looks like a little twat. Like a strawberry Dunkin' Donut Donald. It is on the minds of many and so it would be lovely if you could include this in one of your press conferences or live feeds. If when you talk we could get a close-up of your mouth exposed as the little asshole it is. Get the camera up close and see the hot pink round mouth hole.

We would also like to see you say "go fuck yourself" or "you are fucked." It would be a great media opportunity for high ratings. We are also wondering if it would be possible for a nonstop Twitter marathon. Would it be possible for you to add Facebook Live or YouTube Live so we could be with you in your bed at 3:30 am as you tweet? We wonder, if Melania is beside you, if she could be scantily dressed? Or if you are on the couch looking over the big city, or in the Lincoln office while you are tweeting—upset, in turmoil, furious, exasperated? Just asking, because we want to see your face and get more intimate with you. In fact, if you

could keep the live feed in your bed or in your shorts so
we could see for ourselves that it is working just fine, folks.
We would appreciate the constant contact. We are open to
Twitter toilet time.

THE RED TIE

A legal scholar at Stanford, Thompson Ford argues that Trump's long ties are a desperate show of manhood. "Trump's symmetrical but overlong tie stands out like a rehearsed macho boast, crass and overcompensating," Ford writes, comparing the ties to an overstuffed codpiece.

Cut down the middle
Like two sides of me
Inside
The red striped torso
My innards marked
The red ribbon wrapping
My belly too
The red line
I redline myself
Left to right
My border my heart
My landing strip
Seeing red

DIC PICS, OR, THE CASE OF ANTHONY WEINER

Let me take a pic
Of my dick
Please look at me in all my glory
See me for me
So what? Who cares?
Let me tell you about
The dick pic the dick click tock tick
It isn't the dick pic I tell you
It's the where I am, all of me
For you

Please let me see your masculinity on view in full physical arousal that you are aroused without me being there but at the thought that you will see me. You are awakened that I will "appear" from nowhere. I will come on your screen as you open. I can be deleted or saved and taken away but it is in that moment of disgust of shock like a trench coat I wear on a subway but maybe it is just an image just a moment that occupies my daily desires, my run, so that I can be the man I want to be the man you want me to be
See it, look at it
Play with me

Please, with courtesy, can't we have a space for this member to be able to show his penis pictures in this millennium? For sure, we are all so damn provincial

A hobby, a friendly reminder of the friend between his legs

Do you want to see a dick pic?

I don't think you ever asked and you certainly didn't
    say please.

But it is so lovely and generous that you have done this for
    the nation

For all the voters to see

Here is my dick

Your wiener

Standing at attention

Mark this unfortunate name

I stand like a dunce in the corner wearing the cap
    with wiener

Walking in the school courtyard the target of shame

In the locker room, I heard the Trump locker room talk—

Here is my dic pic

I want to run for mayor my wife is the right arm for
    Hillary, the presidential contender

And I gave you our baby in sext view as a clue

as I was called *baby arm* —monster, rooster and cock a
    doodle doo

As a school boy

Every time I was called "wiener" in class—a laugh

"Weiner, what do you think? Weiner, did you do your
    homework? Weiner, can't you keep up? Weiner, wiener,
    wiener!"

Or I was told to put *it* away

Mother with her staring angry eyes

Averting her gaze after bath play

Friend stayed in my hands still warm and the tension released

Added to put away the shame the shrill the thrill the
    cruelty spilled

But returned to the school yard the next day at play

Weiner wiener pants on fire!

What election process?

What was part of my progress, my own gun control
    legislation

To snap my selfie hoodie woody viewing boxer whites'
    display

Glimpsed for the voters review

Yes, it works! The wiener works!

Please reject me if I

In wishing to be pornography

Desired a Weiner pin-up

Let me get my phone
Ready to snap
Selfie of boxer brief
What were the ones deleted?
I made the best selection for my composition
To share, how generous I am with my endowment
It wasn't impulsive but compulsive
To prepare, plan, my personal foreplay
Someone look at me
Momma don't look away

Rush such a rush
In a rush
Put it away
Crush Hush
Hold on Handy
As my wife Huma
Suspects trusts
Hopes wiener will go away

Huma
My wife stayed with us
While I showed my public private dick
I'm such a generous man, a public man

To share my aptitude this way
My wife stayed by my side
Let me test her more
With hard evidence
My hardness, virility, manhood
I want you to see me
And for you to see her
Looking at me
That's part of the turn-on
Not knowing where to go
To look away to understand
To believe the dick will go away
But the wiener is here
The wiener is here
The wiener won't go away
You can't get
away from me

Wiener dog hot dog
Take a bite of wiener
Weiner is not alone for there is:

Prick *Anaconda* BALONEY PONY **Boner Bone** *Meat Popsicle*

SCHLONG *Chubbie* Mother cock a ding a ling **A dick a dock**

A DUCK A DECK A CHECK A CHICK DING DONG DING

`Going to get this witch dead`

Joy Stick TUNNEL OF LOVING *Man muscle* **Love Bunny cotton tail**

A Piece a Plumber a Joint Schlort Schmeckle *Skin Flute Stiffie*

TALLY WACKER TROUSER MEAT *Winken Weenie Wee* wee wee

Big Piggie all the way home PEENIE WIENIE PEONY PEE

ON ME **IT'S WIENER TIME!**

Let's start again:

Fireman Fire Engine Fire Pole Burrito Beaver Basher

Bishop Broomstick ready for my witch to fly **Light my**

candle aglow `Cum Gun Dagger Custard Load`

Dipstick Dragon Drumstick EASY RIDER EGGROLL

EXCALIBUR FANCY FERRET FIRE HOSE *Creamsicle*

Fudgsicle Popsicle Banana and Lickety Split

LIZARD LONGFELLOW MEMBER *Meter Long King Kong Dong Microphone*

MIDDLE STUMP MOISTURE HEAT-SEEKING VENOMOUS THROBBING PYTHON OF LOVE

Mr. Knish Mushroom Head   *Mutton Old Boy Old Man Old Fellow Old Girl*   **ONE-EYED MONSTER, SNAKE, WEASEL**   YOGURT SLINGER PECKER PEDRO PEEPEE   *Percy Tree Popeye, Sailor Man, Spinach-Time* Pied Piper Pork   **Sword Purple Helmeted Warrior** LOVE QUIVER BONE   *Private Eyed Private Part Prick*   **Dick Tracy Get in my Car** *Big Bird Nookie* `Monster Womb Broom`

Weinis Love-Gun   **Chubby Fun-ster**   *Purple-headed Meat Hammer*   **RICHARD** HIS HERS THEIRS OURS YOURS   *My Johnson Ding Dong Doodly*   **Vanilla from Manilla**   **Dingus Dangus Fudge Packer Holy Diver** *Moses (parts the pink sea)* `Baby Jesus Villy Vonka Vonkey Vrench` SEXY-TUBE MAGIC-STICK LONGSHANKS   *Get off my Bozack*   *Pile Driver, Meat Flute, Hustle Muscle*   **Alabama Black Snake Python Heavy D and the Boys** *Tonsil Tapper the D Vitamin D Get It Right*

OUCH MAKER LOVE LADLE KNIFE *3 Best Friends*

Juice Crew Inflatable POO JABBER *Wedding Tackle* **Slime**

Spitting Flesh Monster Dick Stick Make It Quick *Trouser Tumor*

Mr. Long Skin *Boy Flesh Bat (with balls included)* KICKSTAND FELLA

Quick Draw McGraw *Arrow Meat Thermometer* **St Francis of ASSissi**

Dingypoo PANTSDRAGON **Captain Thick** *Free Willy*

Crank Ninny (when will u ever learn to aim your Ninny better?)

VON LONGSCHLONGSTER BETTY COCK-IT **Drilling Tool Eleventh Finger**

Thor's Hammer *Aretha Franklin Respect Yourself*

Missile Pocket Rocket **LEBANESE SAUSAGE** *Gaza Strip*

Eiffel Tower *Twinkie Ying Yang* Wing Wang Doodle MEAT

AND 2 VEGGIES TOOTER MOOSE *Mr. Moose Captain*

Kangaroo **Scooby Doo Lassie Rin Tin Tin** Barney

Mr Rogers coming to the neighborhood *Piece* Darth Vader

PORK STEEPLE ONE-EYED WILLY *Pocket pud Herman the One-eyed*

German YIPPEE ROD DEW PISTON JUNK DRIVER

CAVE DIVER *Thomas the Tank Trouser Mowzer One eyed*

hound **Flying Purple Pussy Eater Blood Hound**

SHENANIGAN MAKER DRAMA QUEEN Ol Babel Old
Faithful Fat ol' Dick HEDDA GABLER GABLE GOBBLER Dr. Peeper

SPUNK TRUNKET HANG DOWN Blue jean Bazooka Poke
Out Pokey Mon Pokey Man Mr Happy Fatty Fun Gun Flipster
Family Jewels Bird Dirty Hairy Trouser Trout
WEAPONS OF ASS DESTRUCTION WEAPONS OF ASS
DISTRACTION PINK STINGER MEAT DRAGON
TREASURE WING DING BEEF STICK BEST FRIEND Hard on Hot Beef
Injection Lil Buddy Phallus Palace Red Rocket Glare Unit

Velvet Hammer Wood Dangling Diver BUBBA PLUMP STRIPPER POLE
BUSTHEVA HER WEAVE KILL LACE FRONT MASSACRE
Female Popsicle Cucumber Foot Long Fancy Free
Sugar Daddy Sugar Dandy Pickle Sweet Stallion
WOMENATOR SWIPE SHAFT FRANK 'N' BEANS
Corndog Capt. Cave Man Mighty Mouse Pipe Power Drive the
Destroyer MAGIC STICK MANDINGO KING KONG DONKEY
PISTOL PETE QUICK DRAW Scorpion Tail Cinder Fire-breathing Dragon

Monkey Gun Fuck Rod *Muscle Hog Hose Jack Hammer Jimmy*

John Joystick King Lays Rockets Leaking Hose

LITTLE ELVIS LITTLE BOB LOVE STRUCK LUIGI

Oboe Piss Weasel Free Willy *Shaft Soldier Steamer Semen-Truck*

Stick Shift Surfboard Tallywanker Tan Banana Tassel Third

Leg Thumper `Thunderbird Thunderwood` *Tinker Todge*

Tonic Tool Twig and Berries Vein Wand Wang Wang Doodle

Wanger Wanker WEENIE WHOOPEE STICK WICK

Wiener WIENER WIENER WIENER *Wiener* **WIENER** Wiener

Wiener Wiener Wiener Wiener Wiener Wiener Wiener Wiener Wiener

`Wiener Wiener Wiener` WIENER **WienerWinerWinner**

Wiener WIENER *Wiener wiener WINNER*

You are a bad boy, put it away

Put that thing away

Your wiener is showing

We should have changed your name to Winner.

SCARAMUCCI

"I'm not Steve Bannon, I'm not trying to suck my own cock. I'm not trying to build my own brand off the fucking strength of the President. I'm here to serve the country."

I'm not
trying to suck my
own cock
Not trying to suck my own cock

Trying to suck my own cock

To suck my own cock

Suck my own cock

My own cock

Own cock

Cock

Cock own

Cock own my

Cock own my suck

Cock own my suck to

Cock own my suck to trying

Cock own my suck to trying not

Cock own my suck to trying not I'm

Cock my suck to trying not I'm

Cock my suck to trying not

Cock my suck to trying

Cock my suck to

Cock my suck

Cock

my

Cock   Cock

Cock suck to trying not I'm   I'm not trying cock

Cock suck to trying not   I'm trying cock

Cock suck to trying   Not Trying cock

Cock suck to   Trying cock

Cock suck   Cock

Cock   Suck cock

Cock to trying not I'm   Suck cock

Cock to trying not   Cock

Cock to trying   I'm not trying to suck my own cock

Cock to   We heard that about you.

Hello, yes, I am dickless in case you haven't noticed but you
have noticed . . . I won't hold it against you! LOL

Yes, I do not but I do I tell you I have a penis—I do not
have a penis, a dick, just like you. But you don't have a womb
a clitoris or baby maker vestibule. But you also don't have
a brain? What will I play with? I assure you I will have fun at
the Oval Desk.

You don't have a dick
I don't have a dick to snap a pic. Let me
Help me Huma!
Command by the absence of you
Shall I over compensate me
Authority over authority
I am your absence

You don't know the
Pain of childbirth the
Fear of the unknown
The mystery of the
Continuous orgasm
Am I evolved?
Did I allow for the big dick?
After all, I could have been more gracious

Does it always have to be about me being
A wife, a mother—oh yes, why didn't I get that?
Can't I identify as a woman in a pantsuit?
Hello, I would like to pull down my pants and show you mine!
Do you have the absence?
The lack of—
When you see me
You see your mother
Your ever-absent father
Your own false fantasy

Hello, where is my mother?
Like a primal scream
Of a mixed tone of pansies
Does my absence
Have you reach for your trigger?
As I write a pause into sleep
When will the day mare
Nightmare wake up
Or be put to sleep?

I am the Boss of the House
Wait till your father comes home
Am I always the nurturer?

When will this world be fair?

When perhaps two women can run against each other,
    not just as a wife, First Lady

Am I always compensating?

Do you see my flaws, my f- laws?

Feminine Flaws

I am no longer on the rag, on my egg cycle

Complete

With my uterus in check

UTERISM

Let me return to the Oval Office

The Womb Room

Let me bake cookies

And weave a rug with

The insignia and paint China

A hostess as Dolly Madison

Treasured First Lady tropes and empress trains

For my wardrobe not remembered for couture

Let me look at the linens and the floral arrangements
    of the tables

Let me cover the mirrors so you aren't reminded of my face

Let me be under constant examination and disgrace

My silk petticoat in ruins

Let me exchange my panties for cotton slider briefs
As I continue to disappoint no matter what

But I want my turn, damn it!
I don't get hot-headed
As a fear, the worst has happened
I was the confidant
I was the spouse
I was the loving supportive spouse
Of a pig

STAMINA

Hillary Clinton: "As soon as he travels to 112 countries and negotiates a peace deal, a cease fire, a release of dissidents, an opening of new opportunities in nations around the world, or even spends eleven hours testifying in front of a congressional committee, he can talk to me about stamina."

My stamina to move, to run
You question
As I out-multitask, out-maneuver
I have more testosterone than you
And a capacity to proceed process progress
We want to see your stamina, your endurance

What you are really saying is
How long can you fuck?
Are you fucked?
Are you fucked?
Or can I fuck you, or I will out-fuck you?
The vigor
To exert for a long long time
Endurance, my ability to stay with the orgasm
Bags under mister eye-job
No fatigue nor rest with my competence
My mare is charged and ready

As your ability to get on your golf cart
Run off-course and not get the job done
You will never be able to catch up with me
The only one you will fuck is yourself
Go fuck yourself

SHE HE

She He
She She She
Constantly referred to as the *She*
He said *She She She*
As if Hillary doesn't have a name
The only *She* on the stage
The She Devil She Wolf
She did that
She didn't do that
She needs to be stopped
She lies
She is a loser
She is crooked
Not straight
Not a straight shooter
Not straight
A dyke inferred
She is
Questioning her as she
Is she enough?
Saying *she* in her presence, as if she is not in the room
As if she is invisible
Speaking of her without her name. just a gender
Every time saying, *she*

Keeps her gender a priority, a handicap
Hillary is originally a man's name
On the Hill A Ree
I'm with her
Now becomes clearer
He *the* Donald
Was originally the name of a duck?
If it walks like a talks like a quacks like a
Oh Fuck!
We're outta luck
That sucks

Imagine if the history of US presidents were
    all women
And after all these women presidents
After several hundred years
It was decided that finally a man would run
And the most inexperienced man without any diplomatic
    service or political experience would run
The first major male candidate
and that was DONALD TRUMP.

If Donald was a woman—she wouldn't be elected. If
    Hillary was a man.

If *she* did it all in heels, in a pantsuit
Going to hell in a handbag
She'd still be doing it backwards.
But Hillary didn't turn backwards when He lurked
Over her with every turn at the debate
Cowering the She with your He
All of us She's knows that He
All too well
And we all wanted She to tell He
To go to Hell
Why didn't She?

WHEN HILLARY TOOK TOO LONG TO PEE AT THE DEBATE

How long do you take to pee?
Put the image in the stall not in a trench
Whip it out and compare to the gents
Washing hands
Hillary stands
In her own stall
With pantsuit in hand, to lessen the crumple
Taking off her jacket, not to get wet with splatter
Unrolling the thin paper
Tissue tangled ripped protection
And laying on the seat
Maybe there is a seat cover
Holding the dear jacket in fear
And taking down her slacks
Making sure the cuffs don't slide on
Floor's pee grease slime
And she shimmies her
Ass out to drop her drawers and wiggles
The elastic maneuvering
With thumbs eyeing her jacket
On the hook on the door she
Straddles the toilet bowl
With legs akimbo
Holding the crotch of silk sateen

While she holds her bladder without a drip
Then the flow immerses and happy not a spray display
Where is her assistant and daughter?
To hold the unlocked door from peekers
Better slip off the pants
For another day
Panty liner strays
She grabs her Spanx and takes a deep breath before
The waist band catches a nail cuticle
She screams at the French manicure but
Reserves her cries for Syria or Iraq
Gentle now the spigot dribbles and she places tissue
Beneath to catch the rain
As the drip continuous
After the birth of Chelsea
Even with Kegel exercises
It was all worth it
All worth it
All worth it
Maybe I should have worn a dress, she doubts
But there was not a choice
Her pear form
Then suffer the smirks at sausage legs
She washes her hands
There are no towels

Only a cold air drier
Oh, wave those hands flash and scurry out
You know they are waiting
Looking at their man watch
Looking at the door
Maybe saying where is she?
Did she get lost?
You know how women are!
Powder her nose
No lipstick on teeth
Upon her return
What took you so long?
They all stare waiting
An abled sigh
They whip it out
In the multiple trough
With other men diddly
Wash his tiny hands
Dry his tiny fingers
By waving it in the air or wiping
On the derriere of some bimbo
Bitch
Before it is eaten
Witch

FAINTING HILLARY

On that September 11 anniversary
Standing heated
Pneumonia
I fainted slowly
Fast for the fainting couch concrete
With a too tight waist
Take my breath away
An orgasmic loss of consciousness
Catch me so
I fall, full from grace
This female guise
This implosion of death
The location let me
Faint for you my sweet desire
Overtaken by the depths of the body
Memory trauma forsaken
Amidst the planes' crash, explosion
At the site of thousands of ashes at my feet
Let me faint for you my desire
Overtaken by heat fire and sun
The overbearing elements of climate
Please release my shock
My temperature shivers
I'm dizzy losing myself with the

Pelvic massage you insist upon
The public passion of the fainthearted
Climax is only realized by your
Knowledge of my body capacity captivity
As a once New York Senator
Saving
Heroine
Arriving at the scene of Ground Zero
But you only can see me
As a dizzy hyena, a bitch in heat
We have all heard it said
Let me lose loose conventions
Find me catch this fainted form
The power of pussy still thrills
Even in the advent of catastrophe
Let me faint for you
Ever so faintly
At the sight of memory tremor and terror
For a nation
And a war I supported
A notion of my own twin tower
Blown up exploded
Fainted fall down
Before our very eyes

A war I supported
And weapons of mass destruction
didn't question
my horror
collapse
Before my very
eyes

Dear Mrs. Clinton,

We are very pleased to be able to give you some suggestions in regard to your appearance and the way you present yourself. We have evaluated the impression and impact of your choice of wearing a pantsuit. We have taken random polls of how to present the female body in dressing the part as presidential candidate. Here are a few strategies for you and your team to consider:

1. The Tied Down Skirt

    Considering the typical public response "she doesn't know how to dress." We have decided that to make it worse is the way to go.

    Wear a skirt made out of only red ties. But there could be variations. Thinking of the ugly sweater, we suggest you start The Ugly Tie Skirt Campaign. Or ask the nation to send you their ties or husband's, etc. Or have designer tie ensembles. We are hoping this will be a welcome handicraft—something you sorely need. This could help alleviate your preference for US domestic policy over domesticity. If you want to play the woman card, keep it in home issues. We also envision long vests constructed of ties, too. Hopefully, everyone will be talking about the tie outfits with purpose, recycling, and memory.

2. Accessories

   a. What's wrong with your lips? Wear red lipstick. The problem is that you wear neutral shades and that is a concern —neutrality on a woman's mouth.

   b. Carry a purse. It is important that you have some type of enclosed purse and "perform" when you arrive that you need to put "it" somewhere. We want to see you carry the bag on stage and then wonder where to put the damn thing. We suggest that you have the Gold Bag—or Platinum. Coach is very interested in designing a series of Gold Going Presidential Purses and there would be editions for the public but there would only be a particular version for you. H&M likes it too. But theirs will be for tweens.

3. Undergarments

   a. You have done too well in never having an underwear moment. We suggest that on occasion, such as once every three weeks, there is a lapse with a bra strap.

4. Alternatives to the Pant Suit

   a. The biggest complaint or suggestion we have gotten is that you should wear lace with your pantsuit. Go a little Edwardian with lacy shirts. Or we thought that you could have your own puffy shirt, and over vest with the jacket. Would you be opposed to lamé? We thought it be fun if we could create a Hillary Puffy Shirt and then create a campaign ad with your face and voice superimposed on Jerry Seinfeld's. There is a lot to work with here. And we think we can get it played on *Saturday Night Live*. There is nothing like being the target of a joke—well, we don't have to tell you about that!

5. The Belt

Finally, we realized what you are missing is the belt. We know that you have accomplished a lot in your life but if you aren't wearing a belt it doesn't matter. All of the other candidates are guaranteed to be wearing a belt. But even if you are wearing one, the public doesn't know and that is a big problem. *This has been a horrendous oversight.* The belt has to be either black or brown leather with a gold or silver buckle. Simple. Then you need to tuck it all in. We are going to leave that to you, what you will tuck in. We thought you should have some agency here in terms of wardrobe.

We look forward to hearing your thoughts and working with you in being taken seriously! Really looking forward to discussing hair and nails next.

Very truly yours,

The Team at Fashion Political Consultants and Gender

THE MAGNIFICENT OBSESSION (OF THE DELETED EMAILS)

*"Russia, if you're listening, I hope you're able to find the 30,000
emails that are missing."*

A

Deletion gone commando

Castration complex obsession

55,000 pages of emails

The size of it!

30,000 deleted emails on her *personal server*

The *personal server* in the bedroom, revered like some
long-forgotten castrato

Eunuch guarding her chamber

The female candidate deleted her male without our
consent

A transgression a violation a rape

Her emails, shall we say are our *emales*

Removed erased obliterated canceled

Ripped torn brutally callously viscously violently
vehemently desecrated

Erased obliterated canceled

Deleted

Full terror of the castrating bitch

Dreading the castration complexity complicity

Shame on you

I am Evil Devil Woman

Servers slept in a room of linens, dust ruffles, feather
    bed shams

In the privacy of her/my quarters

With a panicked full-alarm fear

Sworded dildos sliced the emales from being found out

Whether Benghazi, a yoga routine, or Bill's infidels

$675,000 in speaking fees with Goldman Sachs

My god, the lady has money on her own.

Reserved as unthinkable, banned and forbidden

Bring Hillary to prison, tried and punished in solitary

Torture her for crimes against inhumanity and indignation

Get her out of that pastel pantsuit and into stripes, an
    orange one-piece

Picking up trash on the side of the road

Or as part of a chain gang

Or in a dungeon—leather, chaps, and chains

Tethered, waxed, tarred, and feathered

With Trump as master, Hillary as submissive

Get her to scream

I am sorry

I am horrible

We can see the porn now

Emales and Punishment
Look who's
Getting sucked off
And that's the way it is.

B
Confine and Stop the Overpowering Deletion Exploits!
Stop Hillary and her email secrecy
In any way possible
See the anguish when taboo is interrupted
In child development: the sexual interest in the mother, a feared
    castration by the father of the son. The mother is blamed when
    she removes her presence . . .
Proves pandemonium is in the air!
Off with your heads!
Off with your emails!
Off with your prick!
She deleted the emales
Her personal emales
And she does it without a dick
But boy does she have balls

Bring this to a vote!
In the privacy of your booth

Oh, this election process
Is some phallic-latent stage
Some penile forfeiture
Kastration angst
And PUTIN put in his dick
I like PUT IN
I would like better relations with PUT IN
I would like better relations with Putin

We are all aware of the difference
Between our legs
And our Hillary, hers has been taken
And if we love her, as mother or virgin and hussy won't do
Then a witch and hag and crone
If we show our love and adoration too much
Bill will take our vulnerable potency away
And of course, symbolically, a metaphor
Not to be eliminated
And not to be dominated
Or to be thought of as unimportant
The extreme focus:
She removed the emales
To keep her autonomy
Above everything else

An irrational move
Against the irrational Trump
The authority is to be his, all his alone
She is simply too dangerous.

C

The Big C

Do they both suffer from castration anxiety?

Do we suffer from castration complex?

In the Oedipal complex we want our mother, all of her, yet we
can't show this desire, so we denigrate and disregard her and
never show respect.

Hillary is not there for Donald
Or is she?

Does or doesn't Hillary know her place within his
complex?

In our Electra complex?

We are initially attached to Hillary—even Trump supported her,
invited her to his wedding. But when she stands side-by-side
with Trump, we prove to DT that no matter how awful he is,
the crueler he is to Hillary, the more jubilancy adheres to this
rigid pyscho-sexual system. He holds the dick, and we don't
want her to take his dick.

Donald's grandiose ambition

Continuous desire for over production
Building with his name on everything!
The completion and physical manifestation
Phallocentrism
(His investments in desire are not very sexy at all)

The computer as a body without genitalia
That holds all the emales
Conquering with opportunity, the email provider empire
For world domination and control
The ability of the world web interior to not be able to
    control information,
The inventory of messages in the emales
Contain and control and destroy the value of a web trail
The emale castrator
Communication with you is threatened
Power is questioned
With full sanction
*What is the fucking big deal? There have been male authorities
    who have deleted before. Is it her seemingly casual unawareness
    of him, her lack of remorse for her deletion/ castration? Like
    some search through Salem for regret and remorse.*
Hillary is an archetypical symbol
She represents what is feared, loathed as the uncaring mother

Her biggest crime is that she didn't recognize Donald

There was no exchange

A cold shoulder

She was never "excited" to see him

She refuses to enter his system of female exchange rate
     with legs lips boobs complete adoration

She has no value

As mother, virgin or whore

He wants to be able to let us know he can fuck her

but she never looks at him, she castrates him

And she is going to suffer.

D

For the Donald

It has happened before

The shrinking penis

Genital shrinking anxiety

Capitalism was built on it

Penis production Over production

What were the bankruptcies all about?

With coldness, the penis will recede into the body

A retraction from the cold shoulder the chilled woman
     the mother

To cause some unnatural death

The removal of emails from the genital-less computer
Could kill us all and is dangerous
Coldness can cause shrinkage
Hillary's coldness can cause retraction, disapproval
We need reassurance (Trump needs reassurance)
In medieval times men could have their penises magically vanish
by witches
Decapitation castration
Oh horror!
Your overcompensation explained
The intimidation, the driving away of disgust
and shame
Apotropaic magic to ward off the evil eye
Turn away all evil influences
But the evil woman remains
A grotesquerie
The grotesque emblem of Hillary
Seen as the head of Medusa
But Donald reminds us he still owns the orange phallus
Magnificent possession not to be tampered with
Providing comfort with his display of grandiosity
His name on every tower and peak
Tangerine stupidity speaks

D IS FOR DISTANT

Hillary becomes the cold distant woman, the mother who
    resists his yearning, longing, desire, and lust
Hillary manages to exert both mother and father
And this displaces Bill, father
We don't know how to see him now
Only as emasculated from power and position
A eunuch amongst us

Donald loves to grab pussy for it confirms that the girl lost
    her penis
And he has to make sure

Hillary is our phallic woman
Seek and suck the penis in the woman
But Hillary's problem is that she is not phallic enough!
Hillary doesn't wear her phallus for Donald, like he
    demands
In a bare leg and tight thigh
With heels, high in a tight erect bound foot
The bare arms cylinder
Long neck with a ribbed choker
Long hair, shafts of hair extensions
A bubble head

To soften the impact of the fear of looking
At the penis–as phallic mother mama
The self as phallus
The boyish girl
Or girlish boy
But there was no gun
No gun no gun
No gun
No penis
Phallic girl Melania, Ivanka, and all the Trumps
Or as one of the boys

Maybe someday there will be a femme fatale head of state
But we are all too phallocentric
When that pussy shine sheen suit
Was never trying to be a man but rather
Look closely it is
Vulva vulva vulvacentric
Hillary is all vulva
Vulva all the time

Or perhaps
Maybe Hillary could be a person
Not defined by genitalia

Try it
You'll like it

Donald wake up
You have womb envy
Jealous glee over ovary justice
Of the gendered system
Forced to reproduce and overproduce
That is how you make your money
Your own form of production
Just remember entering possessing
Leaves you withered
To make a man less than a man
To make a man less than man
Humiliation
Don't bring up your anal expulsive personality
Let's not go there.

Hold up to a mirror to read this mysterious letter.

Dear Messrs Chairmen:

In previous congressional testimony, I referred to the fact that the Federal Bureau of Investigation (FBI) had completed its investigation of former Secretary Clinton's personal email server. Due to recent developments, I am writing to supplement my previous testimony.

In connection with an unrelated case, the FBI has learned of the existence of emails that appear to be pertinent to the investigation. I am writing to inform you that the investigative team briefed me on this yesterday, and I agreed that the FBI should take appropriate investigative steps designed to allow investigators to review these emails to determine whether they contain classified information, as well as to assess their importance to our investigation.

Although the FBI cannot yet assess whether or not this material may be significant, and I cannot predict how long it will take us to complete this additional work, I believe it is important to update your Committees about our efforts in light of my previous testimony.

Sincerely yours,
James B. Comey, Director

CLEANING UP BILL'S MESS

I cleaned up his shit
His piss his cum
Her puss her gas her ass
His pass
Cleaning up his mess
His bitch
His switch
His twitch witch bitch
Pass it on
Give me a wink
For the twink
Clean up after twink—wink wink
I think, please eat her on the mink
The stink of pink kink link
What a fink on the brink
Sink stink stink
Prick shrink pink kink wink link
Shrink
See a shrink

Cleaning up after Bill
Oh, I cleaned up
Oh, baby I cleaned up good
Speeches at $300,000

Corporate and foreign donations
A little uranium
To the foundation
Something with Haiti
And UBS

Back and forth
The messes, misses, masses
What about the relationship to Bill and his mess?
Uh, yeah
What is the relationship to the Donald always making
    a mess?
Uh, yeah
Hillary cleaning up her mess, duh
A big hot fucking *put-it-in-the-bank* mess. That'll work.
The men of finance—making a mess out of things–
    cleaning it up
Cleaning up the ooze, the goose, give me the booze
Lose the sweet smell of sweet success mess
Since the beginning of time

But bring it back to our president
Orange mess White House
Needs to be wiped

Come in and wipe me
Oh, no leaks!
Embedded held and withdrawn
The messy Twitter attacks
Uncontrollable urges
Explosion turds
Like some high-speed accident
A DUI
Making in his pants
Bringing in the clean undies
To school
You smelly smelly boy
I didn't mean to
Hold it in next time
Hold it in
Mommy Daddy poopy
To disavow, spoil
Have a sulk fit
The spoiling-the-fun runs
Make a mess out it
Spoiler alert alarm
You are a dirty boy
Such a dirty dirty boy
Cause damage

Make a mess

Making a mess out of it

Anal retentive

Anal expulsive

Spoiling outburst

Uncontrollable outburst

What a terrible boy

Don't say that you wail

A smelly boy

Keep the poopy in

Retention rates

Can't you feel the signs of your own body

Fecal holding awareness with practice

Watch for the leaks

The leakers leak

Who's making a poopy?

Who's making the leaks?

Be the real asshole

Be a real asshole

Don't take anyone's

Shit

Even at the inauguration

Taping over the name on the potty

Don's Johns.

WORD JUMBLE: FIND BILL'S LADIES

```
Q R C S G T A O W V K D L R T H E G
D O L L Y K Y L E B R O W N I N G E
I W Y R C W N E V Z M G V L M D Q N
K E O Q K K D L C W J Z Q H O N W N
A V S M H A B V G T P B H K N L M I
J U A N I T A B R O A D D R I C K F
R Q L Z H H L N G R U L X O C P C E
A L L H G L N M T W L C J E A T P R
U E Y X P E Y E P O A H I B L N Q F
L E P I Q E P N C A J L W T E Z X L
C N E B Z N E G J I O B M Q W V M O
F D R G M W R K C N N A S E I V U W
L O D X R I D E W G E L H T N N S E
O S U M F L U T B P S K Q N S T B R
R L E Q B E G T H K V N L E K I R S
S X L T N Y Q X D O E W S R Y O K T
H E L I Z A B E T H G R A C E N L W
E W G R A D H Z W O J P M A D R C O
```

Juanita Broaddrick; Dolly Kyle Browning; Gennifer Flowers; Paula Jones;
Elizabeth Gracen; Monica Lewinsky; Sally Perdue; Kathleen Wiley

IF ONLY

If only she said she liked to grab men by their balls
maybe she would have had a chance
If only she had five children by three husbands
maybe she would have had a chance
If only she went bankrupt several times
maybe she would have had a chance
If only she created a fake university and ripped off students
maybe she would have had a chance
If only she didn't pay income tax for years
maybe she would have had a chance
If only she wasn't a nasty woman
maybe she would have had a chance
If only she said her daughter had a hot bod
maybe she would have had a chance
If only she imitated a disabled person
maybe she would have had a chance
If only she painted her face orange and wore a red tie and
    looked like a clown
maybe she would have had a chance.

MATTHEWS: *OK, here's the problem—here's my problem with this. If you don't have a punishment for abortion—I don't believe in it, of course—people are going to find a way to have an abortion.*

TRUMP: *You don't believe in what?*

MATTHEWS: *I don't believe in punishing anybody for having an abortion.*

TRUMP: *OK, fine. OK.*

MATTHEWS: *Of course not. I think it's a woman's choice.*

TRUMP: *So you're against the teachings of your church?*

MATTHEWS: *I have a view—and a moral view. But I believe we live in a free country, and I don't want to live in a country so fascistic that it could stop a person from making that decision.*

TRUMP: *But then you are...*

MATTHEWS: *That would be so invasive...*

TRUMP: *I know, but I've heard you speaking...*

MATTHEWS: *So determined of a society that I wouldn't be able— one we are familiar with. And Donald Trump, you wouldn't be familiar with.*

TRUMP: *But I've heard you speaking so highly about your religion and your church.*

MATTHEWS: *Yeah.*

TRUMP: *Your church is very, very strongly, as you know, pro-life.*

MATTHEWS: *I know.*

TRUMP: *What do you say to your church?*

MATTHEWS: *I say, I accept your moral authority. In the United States, the people make the decision, the courts rule on what's in the Constitution, and we live by that. That's why I say.*

TRUMP: *Yes, but you don't live by it because you don't accept it. You can't accept it. You can't accept it. You can't accept it.*

MATTHEWS: *Can we go back to matters of the law and running for president because matters of the law, what I'm talking about, and this is the difficult situation you've placed yourself in.*

By saying you're pro-life, you mean you want to ban abortion. How do you ban abortion without some kind of sanction? Then you get in that very tricky question of a sanction, a fine on human life, which you call murder?

TRUMP: *It will have to be determined.*

MATTHEWS: *A fine, imprisonment for a young woman who finds herself pregnant?*

TRUMP: *It will have to be determined.*

MATTHEWS: *What about the guy that gets her pregnant? Is he responsible under the law for these abortions? Or is he not responsible for an abortion?*

TRUMP: *Well, it hasn't—it hasn't—different feelings, different people. I would say no.*

MATTHEWS: *Well, they're usually involved.*

IT'S MY BODY

Women should be punished
Go to jail for abortion
Trump said
Some form of punishment if abortion was illegal
The woman's body controlled
The woman must be a mother
She will be punished
If she isn't a mother she will be jailed
Over her dead body

It is my body
It is not Trump's body
It's not Pence's body
It's not Session's body
It's not Cruz's body
It's not Melania's body
It's not Ivanka's body
It's not Bill's body
It's not Hillary's body
Legislated
It's not
It's not the court's body
It's not the Pope's body
This body is mine

You will not jail me
You will not own my body
I will not be punished
Women
Legislate
Their own
Bodies and destiny
It's my body
It is not your body
My body

THAT ANAL STAGE

Look at my blossom brim
Strained rosebud lips
Pursed squeezed mouth
Pushing out shit speak
squeezing a morning froth
Nothing like spewing a tweet latte
More like triple expresso
My expressive toilet screams beckon
Push so hard to get it all out
All the shit poo mess mess out of me
I am your asshole
Your smooth move
Oral obstruction, verbal siege
Crapola Crayola in any color
Your number 2
As mommy waits for me to do my smelly doo doo
I won't I won't I holler and scream
I hold it in but then it just bursts out mean
I just can't help myself
I had an accident so to speak
Unexpectedly that spoken outrage
Mean mommy
Bad boy
I didn't make a press mess

It is all fake news
Unacceptable forbidden
You lie

Let me purse my trap
Into a ground-around rosy
Round-about asshole
My very own pussy perineum frame
Let me speak a shout out to
All the crap expletives
No worries I will just flush it down the drain
Bye bye poo poo stains
Mommy will never look at
From this vantage view
Discharging disgusting
So disgusting so disgusting so disgusting
So disgusting so disgusting

Let me tell a lie
Or be very mean and crude
Let me cut you off
Offensive filthy insulting
Let me say the most terrible things
Horrific cruel mean sadistic

Outrageous infuriating lewd
Disturbing inappropriate rude
Revolting repulsive repellant
Just so full of shit

My rounded pucker barks
Ready to defecate sparks
The brown messy a hot brown
Ready to push the turd
Fuming media mommy at my mess
Furious White House staff alert
So irritated and livid
So frustrating and irritating
Please don't make a mess
Please hold it in
Please don't tweet

A smelly relief
Sometimes hard
Or liquid gravy
And when the crap
Hold it in hold it in
Hold it in
Can't can't can't
Then it's time to tweet

Oh sweet tweetness
Have a tantrum temper delirium
Have a convulsion spasm
Make it all go away
Push this turdy out
And drain this putrid swamp

Bursting at the instant gut
Let me twit twat Twitter
Let it out let it out
Shit on me automatic narrative nerve
My mouth anus famous verb
Glory hole hollow story hour power
Spoken gaseous gab glee gallow
Fart talk redemption retreat
Taking the vapor out of the room
Melt away disembowel follow
Dripping slime diarrhea talk stalk
Corrupted irritable bowel syndrome
Shit storm in here please
Hate when shit happens
Rump with no T
Such a smelly dirty boy
I guess draining the swamp
Starts with me.

ON LIVING WITH THE NAME TRUMP

You are such an ass
That RUMP
Let me take a dump Trump
Not triumphantrump
But a bastard baby of a Scottish nanny
Domestic territory, clean it up Scottie
Trump dump table scraps
Little rump nappy SAD
Pin the tail on the trump boy
We can also presume
wet the bed assume
LEAKING
Leakers
Escape release and ruin
Golden shower play

We can hear baby Donny
If only I could love mommy
If only mommy could love me
Shit slut shut
Son of bitch twitch rich
Ass hat wipe
You never wipe right
Even with your White House tissue

Caught on toes tucked under shoes
Crack butt idiot names refuse
Jerk pig schmuck hurt too

Here comes Trumplestiltskin
That A Hole
Stallion posterior position
Ass clown ass mug ass menagerie
Ass mush ass swipe Ass ATM Bite
Chump chunk change of stool
That Humpty Dumpy Trumpy
Sat on a wall and fell
And all the king's men
Couldn't fix him

Big bag of shit bastard bat fastard
Bo Beep face bia-biatch
All business keep it business
DO YOUR BUSINESS
Imagine all the names you've been called
Walk the dog poop and scoop
Blank stick bottom feeder caboose
Buttzilla on the run—push it buffalo bun
A big animal parade pie to step on

A buffoon a bugaboo a bugapoo
Bugger butt, butt-head butt mush
Butt plug chicken head chad
Choade monster chute and
Ladders russet clump cluster
Bronzed drizzle stick constellation
Cock cunt somewhere here
Devil dick dirty rag drag
Dick face bun run Fanny got my gun
Drill hole dirty boy douche bag gooze
Dazzle frazzle gobble goober shooter
A donkey a jackass hole blow
Lame blame ass
TRUMPRUMPDUMP
Mother trucker fucker
Pickle Purple pucker pita plucker
Poop head Peter eater
Scrub sack rat hide scag
Scum bag scum bucket
Shit face rump trump
Dump a doodle doo
Sick fuck skag
Sleaze ball snatch
Stool box pantry

Wanker room tidy waste

Garbage din compost pile paste

Turdy gurdy man taste

My name is rump with a

T

Or Dump for short

This asshole can never help itself

Butt of jokes

Buttered up roll butt

Ass kisser, ass whisperer, ass shouter, ass without conditions

Asshole attacks shrieks

Here comes Mr. Nasty

Can't say nothin' nice

Rump trump dump roast

Bunghole buttocks Butt tucks

Backside Rectum

Lower opening of the digestive tract

Rear end hind gutter

Inwards kishkies

Here comes the shit

Orifice bottom

I am a colon cleanser

Time to tweet

And toot some loose
Enema inner mechanism
Trump is here and clear
Lying on folds between buttocks
Oh sweet sweet LYING

Butthole cecum duodenum Fanny pack gizzard guts Pylon
tickers abdominal anal Anatomic structure that opens rectum
Back passage bung buns Entrails foregut giblet Insides out
intervals intestine Lower opening of the alimentary midgut
Opening of the lower end rectum Opening opposite end
digestive tract Outlet terminal end love canal

The behind breech opening
Rectal stiffen
Tripe trips tips rips
Vent vernacular appendix
Viscera vitals works
Not heart kidney
But blind gut reason
The cauldron bottom opening
Pumps abdominal case back
Colonic cry

Pump dump rump trump

Derriere duodenal dyspeptic

Esophagus excrement fundamental

Gullet, hepatic hind end

Kettle bottom

Pepsin portal

Seat shit sob sad

So sad

Sad turd

Get a grip

Give me mean and nasty

Trump's speaky smelly

Tail tail-end talk talk wail

Tramp trump tush

Liver flush no lights

Giving the moon

Where the sun don't shine

Small intestine

Neighbor spleen and stomach

Bastard dickhead bad digestion

Pepto Bismol, Alka Seltzer no relief

Nothing works except expulsion

Can't help myself need to clear the air
Say something foul odored
tweet

Heartburn hindquarters
Hobo juice 24-hour flu all the time
Gushing Montezuma's revenge
I need the wall against Montezuma's Revenge
The wall I need against my terror poo tweet
Metabolic mother fucker
This shit is mine!
ALL MINE
Talking shit
Can't take this shit
Eating shit

Full of shit

It's a disaster
I shit I shit a long time
Talking shit
This is my shit
For I'm worth nothing but shit
Shit hole

Dunghill manure heaps
Mouths off
Turds buffalo chips
Cow chips and flogs
Tool fool crap bull
Night soil meanie coprolite
Fossilized feces found
Defecation dingle berry
Dirt dung fart feces filth
I can't help myself
Guava mauve sauce
Here it comes out
Orifice scandal
Expressive sewage shit speak
Creamed dinner
Soul slimer
It's a disaster
Oh, the leaks start here!
Tweet

Dropping smelly insults
Assholes bastard cowpats poop
Loser
Loser

Can't get off the bowl
Mother of all bowel movements
Bugger bigger angry creep tweet
Some crazy shit is right
Darn diddly dog, dog shit
Feculence flatulence
Stepping in shit all over the house
On the shoe, the dog goo
All over hood hoot jerk louse
Pick up after this dog
Get me a doggie bag
A pooper scooper
It's a disaster
A total disaster
I'm a disaster

Prick pukes rat's ass
Scum shuts stink sink stank stink stink
Snake snot stern stinker stanker retch
Tail toad nincompoop
Shithead daddy squat jack
Low down Let daddy sit on his throne
Small squish squash in between toes
Damn it I stepped in my own shit

Trump dump rump pump poo
You are going to look at that shit
My beautiful ugly shit
It is all mine
Before I flush it down
I don't want to let it go
Just one more Tweet please
Living up to the name of Trump.

TOILET TRAINING

What a disaster
A diss ass turd
Toilet training resistance
Potty mouth
Potty training
Too early too late
Stool holder
Can't help it
The pee and poo belong to you not us
Power struggle
You have the poo now
Mommy said I knew you could do better
Had to run bare bottom
Remove the impacted hard
Release constipation
Dismantle the power struggle
Stool softener rectal signals
You can't watch TV until you have a Twitter
Tweet hard
Tweet and squeeze hard for mommy
Push that tweet
Hold that tweet for mommy
Can't control his sphincter
No potty prodigy

Dumb shit
Dumb tweet
I had a poop accident
Conflict—poop conflict
Parental diarrhea
Coffee enema gush
Can't control the sphincter
Can't control the ass
Child has no control
Over his own bowels
This is some crazy ass shit
Trump
That's how this RUMP rolls
What a dump
This White House is such a dump.

CONFESSIONS OF COVFEFE

Covfefe
Is when I fuck it up
And then I fuck it up more
And undo the fuck
To relive the fuck

Covfefe is when I fall asleep
In the middle of a fuck
And awaken not remembering what the fuck

Covfefe is a cluster double fuck
Such as when I fuck up the deal in climate change
And then say fucked up things to a London mayor at the
    time of a terrorist attack

When will I ever shut the fuck up?
Covfefe begins with a *con*
A deceit
And the middle with a *v*
For vagina
And ends with *fefe*
A fefe is a rolled towel
Placed in a rubber glove
With a sock over rubber to keep in place

Add warm water
And slip your dick in
Hand job in prison
Hmm
A deceit vagina
Lock her up
Covfefe
Is man-made trouble
I would be your Covfefe

Covfefe is an addiction to the smart phone
Dependence on the mobile device
Trump's brother was an alcoholic
And died from the disease
Covfefe is bottoming out
The phone, social media, checking, posting
Texting as an addiction
Mobile phone dependency
The phone becomes the drug, the binge drinking
The out of control behavior
The drunken verbal assault
The pussy, the handjob, the all night can't stop
Uncontrollable covfefe
Bottomed out black out 12 steps

Covfefe stands for

Continued Online Violations For Extreme Fixated
    Expression

Fixated frustrated

Psychotic disturbance with just one tweet

Cannot have just one tweet

Lonely tweeting alone

Staying home tweeting alone

Panic anxiety

Disturbed relationships at work

Drunk on Twitter mobile device

Dependence syndrome

Just can't stay away from it

Time to come to the realization that you are
    powerless over the tweet

Covfefe.

So nice, thank you very much. That's really nice. Thank you. And it's an honor to have everybody here. This is beyond anybody's expectations. There's been no crowd like this. No crowd like this. [applause] Our country is in serious trouble. *I'm in serious trouble.*

We don't have victories anymore. We used to have victories, but we don't have them. *I don't have victories. I don't have them.* When was the last time anybody saw us beating, let's say, China *Vagina,* in a trade deal? They kill us. *THEY KILL US! THEY ARE KILLING US!* I beat China *Vagina* all the time. All the time.

When did we beat Japan at anything? They send their cars over by the millions, and what do we do? When was the last time you saw a Chevrolet in Tokyo? It doesn't exist, folks. They beat us all the time.

When do we beat Mexico at the border? They're laughing at us *they are laughing at me.* at our stupidity. *At my stupidity.* And now they are beating us economically. They are not our friend, believe me. *I am not your friend, believe me.* But they're killing us economically. *I am killing you economically.* The US has become a dumping ground for everybody else's problems. *I am dumping all my problems.*

When Mexico sends its people, they're not sending their best. They're not sending you. They're not sending you. They're sending people that have lots of problems. *I have lots of problems. I have lots and lots of problems and I am bringing those problems.* And they're bringing those problems with us. They're bringing drugs. *I act like I am on drugs. I need drugs. I am on drugs. Give me some drugs.* They're bringing crime. *Have I committed a crime? I'm bringing crime.* They're rapists. *Just because Ivana accused me of rape in the divorce papers and well,* and some, I assume, are good people. *I'm not a good person.* But I speak to border guards and they tell us what we're getting. *What we are getting? I'm at the border of Trader Joe's, why is there such a line? Why is there a line?* And it only makes common sense. It only makes common sense. They're sending us not the right people. *I am not the right people. I am not the right person.*

It's coming from more than Mexico. It's coming from all over South and Latin America *it's coming from Indiana, it's coming from Atlantic City* and it's coming probably, probably, from the Middle East. But we don't know. We don't know. *I don't know. I don't know. I don't know anything.* Because we have no protection and we have no competence. *I have no competence.*

We don't know what's happening. *I don't know. I don't know. I don't know anything.* And it's got to stop and it's got to stop fast. *I got to stop and I got to stop fast. Stop me. Someone stop me!*

They've become rich. *I'm rich.* I'm in competition with them. And we have nothing. *I have nothing. I have nothing. I have nothing. I am nothing.* We can't even go there. *I can't go there. I can't even go there.* We have nothing. *I have nothing. I am nothing.*

That's right. A lot of people up there can't get jobs. *I can't get a job. I don't know how to do my job. I had* The Apprentice. *I need a job. I didn't have a job. I'm a nut job.* They can't get jobs, because there are no jobs, because China *Vagina* has our jobs and Mexico has our jobs. They all have jobs. *I better keep my job. I don't want to be out of a job.* Our enemies are getting stronger and stronger by the way, and we as a country are getting weaker. *I am getting weaker and weaker and weaker. Weaker. I am so weak.*

When was the last time you heard China is killing us? *Vagina is killing us.* They're devaluing their currency to a level that you wouldn't believe. *I'm devaluing currency. I don't pay my taxes. I go bankrupt.* They're killing us. *I'm killing you. They're killing me. You're killing me.* But Russia. I like Putin very, very much. He is a leader. *I like Putin very, very much. Put it in PUT*

IT IN PUT IN PUT IN PUT IN *I want to get along* RUSH IN *Put In.* RUSH AH! PUT IN! *I like him very much.* Because we have to stop doing things for some people, but for this country, it's destroying our country. *I'm destroying this country.* We have to stop, and it has to stop now. *I have to stop.* I'll bring back our jobs from China, from Mexico, from Japan, from so many places. I'll bring back our jobs, and I'll bring back our money. Because we need money. *I need money. I need money.* We're dying. We're dying. *I'm dying. I'm dying.* We need money. *I need money.* We have to do it. And we need the right people. *Where are the right people? I can't find the right people?*

There may be somebody with tomatoes in the audience. So if you see somebody getting ready to throw a tomato, knock the crap out of them, would you? Seriously. Okay? Just knock the hell— I promise you, I will pay for the legal fees. I promise, I promise. It won't be so much 'cause the courts agree with us too. It's disgusting what's happening to our country. *I'm disgusting I'm disgusting, what I am doing to this country.* We are a dumping ground for the rest of the world. We are a dumping ground. *I am dumping. I am dumping. Dump dump dump.* We have to ban the Muslim people. *We have to ban me. Ban me.*

I would build a great wall. *I need a wall around me so I can't get out.* And nobody builds walls better than me, believe me, and

I'll build them very inexpensively, I will build a great, great wall on our southern border. *My southern border down south needs a wall on my southern border.* And I will have Mexico pay for that wall. *I don't know who is paying for the wall. They'll pay for the wall. I need a wall.*

Because I said I'm going to build a wall and Mexico is going to pay for it, right? First of all, there is going to be a wall. This isn't one of those deals where they jump over it, they go to Home Depot, buy a ladder, jump over the wall.

This is my wall. This is a Trump wall. This is a real wall. *I want a gorgeous wall with my name on it—in lights, in mosaics, stained glass, with golden fixtures, maybe condos at the wall with inside prices for $500,000 including a green card. A casino at the wall, a golf course at the wall. Swimming pool at the wall. The* Apprentice *at the wall. Now that wall is a mall. A border mall. CAN SOMEONE KEEP ME OUT. KEEP ME OUT.*

You know, the Trump wall, that would be a beautiful wall mall. *That's why I have to make it beautiful because some day when I'm gone, they are going to name that wall after me. And Mexico is going to pay. I know they won't pay. And you know we will need to use immigrants to build this wall.*

TAKE THESE STATUES DOWN

ON CONFEDERACY

"Sad to see the history and culture of our great country being ripped apart with the removal of our beautiful statues and monuments."

In keeping these statues
idols of enslavement
a memory trauma lives
ready for battle
oppression
our nation's narrative
holding the bondage shrill
a license to kill
In equaling your bigotry
Support of hate
Comfort to racists
Safe harbor to terrorists
From devil heart

White sheet slave owner
Plantation daddies
who raped
Pillaged black bodies
Creating children to enslave
with master names as property

Bought sold traded flesh
As chattel inherit
And whether as Jefferson
Robert E. Lee
Or Strom Thurmond
Or *12 Years a Slave*

Where is our national memorial?
To commemorate
Educate
Our ugly history
forced brutal violent captivity
What part of this don't you understand?
and these statues carry on fear
There is no shade protection
Tree limbs hold ropes to throat
From Jim Crow's nest
The memory is everywhere
in this landscape rest
cotton or skittles
or no turn signal

Triggered by a determined presence
Constant certain statue idol

Commanding presence
looms proof
when you do not condemn
but condones and inspires
White supremacy
White nationalism
Provides the cruel encounter
Admiring perpetrator on pedestal
From above with profiles against heaven
Instead of dirt

These statues must come down
We will not weep
Tear up as we tear up
the confederate flag
emblems of racism
as you insist
with the evil heart
We resist

Sing up courage now
Take up your humanity fist
Resist white in power fools
Bring these statues down

Tumble marble
bronze broken
Stone collapse
But we must do more
than just remove
The physical
We must
Remove and obliterate the hate
To form a new legacy
Of freedom
Equality and justice for all

Bring these statues down

"Why are we having all these people from shithole countries coming here?"

Welcome to my land that I protect. The land I colonized, stole, occupied, profited from, and reign. The land we need to continue to defend, have dominion over, and keep pure. This land is my land, this land is your land—and let's keep it our land and not their land.

The land that is my earned income birthright from the millions I inherited, through a legacy of profit before people, white power and being a zealot. I did it my way—the white way. Keep it our land. Keep them out.

America is great for we generously allow migrant agricultural laborers a chance at providing for their families—*although not a living wage*—still, we provide the struggle for their meager existence, yet we are the true caretakers of this land. And I am proud of this accomplishment.

After the crops are harvested we must return the exploited, beleaguered workers to where they came from. This earth and our way of living must not be taken over by the crossing of borders to come here and take advantage of our way of life!

Like this rose, cultivated into designed perfection– we need to control the nature of immigration at all costs—we must accept the thorn to enjoy the potential bloom

of the immigrant's toil– with their over-production, their fertility, *their breeding,* their infiltration and penetration. We will legislate authority of what is already ours!

Yes, I am an extremist of white makes right! Yes, I am a fanatic when it comes to upholding what is rightfully mine! Yes, I am a bigot in that my privilege sustains my supremacy. I maintain a required enthusiasm for keeping out the undesirables who wish to multiply and alter our way of life.

The view, the landscape, these mountains, this fertile soil and greenery will not be owned or be hospitable to any marginal, dangerous ethnic types—or any others under my command. Unless they buy a condo or casino from me.

This land is my land. This land is your land. But let's keep it our land!

ANCHOR BABY

I'm an anchor baby
My mother was an immigrant
Melania is an immigrant
Ivana is an immigrant
I have four anchor babies
Donny, Eric, Ivanka, Barron
Maybe I should be deported?
I want to build a wall around me
A wall you will pay for
To not be able to get into me
I'm a bully a narcissist
It's all about me me me
Because all I want is to be on unreality TV
And why are you interested in me?
The same reason you are interested in *Dancing with the Stars*
The same reason you can't get enough of your abusive
    father
Enough of your condescending racist mother
Your overbearing meddling parent
I had a dream that Rosie O'Donnell was sleeping next
    to me
I was such a son of a bitch cruel mean man to her
Somebody stop me! Somebody stop me!

I thought she would stop me
Everything I said about her is really about me.

I am afraid you will find out about my vulnerability
My hair helmet is my vulnerability—my pussy, my page boy,
    my spit curl, my teased hornet's nest, my queen bee hive
Like Twiggy, Eva Gabor in a mink coat, Debbie Harry
    eating at the diner on 23rd Street
I'm with her
I am Madonna riding the elevator at Danceteria
and later in *Desperately Seeking Susan*
I want to be Madonna!
Don't you find me beautiful?
I am the material girl
Why do you hate me so much?
I was looking at myself, playing with my hair, and the hair
    started taking on a life of its own.
A creature, a nightmare
My kinky fetish
My kind of girl
That is why I have to be such a pig, for I am really am
    a pussy
My head is my pussy

My sprayed wiglet, my merkin

I really want to be a Barbie

I want to be Ivana

I want to be Marla

I want to be Melania

I want to be Ivanka

I want to be Hillary

I want to be Megyn

I want to be Mika

Don't mess with my hair

Don't play with my junk

Why are you such a mean son of a bitch, Donald?

Are you afraid to be called a pussy?

I am a fucking pussy

Grab me some pussy

That angry cat

Call me meow

A kitten

A cat

A bowl of warm milk

Soured

Scalded

I am Rapunzel

Climb up my briar rose

See my hair through my window
The breeze behind my halo horns
The blonde bombshell adored
I am Marilyn with JFK
I am stalked by Hitchcock
I am Marie Antoinette
I let them eat cake
I say pardon *moi* at the guillotine
I am Kate Hudson and Goldie
I am the butt of jokes in *Laugh In*
I am the dumb blonde the dirty blonde
Does the carpet match the drapes?
I am Jean Harlow held by Gable in *Hold Your Man*
Gentlemen Prefer Blondes
My hair is Faye Dunaway's running away in *Bonnie
    and Clyde*
My hair is in my face, my eyes as I speak
Like Veronica Lake
Lana Turner, whose daughter killed her lover
Brigitte Bardot with an animal kingdom
I am *Legally Blonde 1 and 2*
I am Cameron Diaz when I smear your jizz on my locks
I am platinum blonde
Marlene Dietrich in *Blonde Venus*

Blonde Trouble

Blond Ambition

I am dumb and dumber and dumbest

I am teased, taunted, and humiliated

As all I want is when I watch your hair on my cock

I want the same chance

To suck some dick with my flowing bedroom hair

With botox frozen grin

My orange salmon face puffed with afterglow

I can't wait to bring my teased face and verbally abuse all
of you more

And have a meltdown and go bankrupt and self-destruct

I am Eva Marie Saint kissing Cary Grant on the train

Ready for Grace Kelly's close-up

Kim Novak in *Vertigo*

I love a Barbie doll wife

And Barbie doll daughters, Tiffany and Ivanka

And you can see the sky as you look through my thinning
mane as

You pray at Trump Tower

Trump Tower is my Flower Power

I can't wait to be Princess Dianna with my short yellow

Racing in the night to get away

I am all blondes

Light ash

Golden

Champagne

Butterscotch

Beeline honey

Dirty trashy dumb blonde

Oh, please let me be Carrie Underwood!

I am a blonde bitch from hell—complaining and sassing

I am your best friend, I am Jennifer Aniston

I am your dominatrix or better your submissive

Baiting you and humiliating you till I am given the wall
    that you pay for

I am Doris Day with Rock Hudson

I am Tippi Hedren as Marnie

Oh Marnie, oh Marnie who can't see red

Don't you see it is all a game

When I said that Megyn Kelly was bleeding

Of course, I'm a liar and a cheat

I want a bleeding pussy

To call my own, that I can remote out of

My own Twitter twatter feed

See me Tweet

My twatter my twat

That I can stick a tampon in

Or sanitary pad below
Where my pubes stick to the paste of tired melted rouge
Am I fucked up enough to be your fearless leader
Don't touch my hair
Don't touch me
I will bankrupt you for free
If you are asking why I ran it was more than the
    twisted power
It was to be running against Hillary
To have the opportunity to publicly shame humiliate
    debase and be cruel
I want to be that blonde and trash her
Be sadistic
Everything I always wanted to say to Momma
Everything I wanted to say to Poppa
You will all pay
A self-destructing narcissist shadow display
And I knew she could take it and she would still show up
    at my inauguration
 She couldn't resist the temptation as I can put up the
    crank
The torture—lock her up. LOCK HER UP
Lock me up
With no worry for a safe word

She is my blonde pantsuit desire

Melania couldn't keep up

I took up where Bill let go

I am everyone she hates and loves

I am her father, her brothers, her mother, her husband,
    the system

The law, authority, transportation, the institution

The weapons

The President

I am everything she is not

Push against me bitch

You can take it

Push against me

Harder Harder Harder

I am the emotional one

I'm the crazy bitch she can control

I want to fuck with you harder harder you can take it

You are the resilient one

Let me do this for you

How much can you take? How much can you take?

I am the hysterical bitch

The post menopause rug rat

The chaos kid

I am the angry hungry taunting cunt

The vagina dentata

Let me be the woman in the pant suit

Let me be hysterical

I am with her

Grab me some pussy

Let me woman up

I am the pussy

I am the angry hungry taunting cunt

The vagina dentata

Let me be the woman in the pant suit

Let me woman up

I am the pussy

Let me be hysterical

I am with her

GRATITUDE

Some musings on the female candidate's emotional state of gratitude

Oh, I need my gratitude apron. I should WEAR my gratitude apron for the world to see my gratitude in full view. Where is my gratitude apron? I should wear the apron of thank-you cards. Wrapping my female frame, my gracious generous hips with a continuous smile of gratitude humbleness embedded on my chest. A thankfulness display that I am able to be here with you now.

I feel so grateful in a way that is beyond my ability to express the gratitude that is here now in this room. I am so grateful for all of you and your support and that every day the knowledge I receive from all of you, all the time with the utmost support that is recalled and envisioned. I am humbled by the ability to be here with you, with all of your talent and thank you so much, thank you. Did I say thank you I am saying thank you I am saying thank you thank you thank you and I am grateful to be here for the privilege to be here with you now and to experience everything by and with you. Your support never ceases to amaze me. Before I forget did I say thank you? You can never say it enough. I don't know why I am here but I do know that I am here to give thanks. I need my gratitude apron.

I am so grateful—not that I am great—but I am great *full*—*full* of greatness. Gratitude is my attitude. I have the attitude with gratitude that I shall speak softer and I will speak in carefully chosen words, enunciate syllables in crafted sentences that just hum off the page. Let me hum that sweet song of gratitude! I am not only grateful but I am very appreciative.

I am grateful, full of gratitude that my seething self-contempt may someday vacate, only to be a whisper. *Whisper whisper gratitude.* I am the gratitude whisperer. I cry. I wail. I shed tears. *Waa waa waa* but I am never too far away to take things for granted. I am dependent on my gratitude, a gratitude dependency. Dependent on the cheery way I smile and look at your beauty that resonates. Oh, you are beautiful. You are looking good. It is always a mystery, this profound thing called living a life in gratitude and deep appreciation. So even if I clench my teeth and do not return your calls and ignore you, I am grateful in my downward dog.

Now for some gratitude memories—

I need to tell you that your energy at the Gluten Free Gourmet was a bit off and so let's stay positive and get to the spiritual ... but of course you owe me money and I think it is your way of getting closer to me—your personal debt, your Karma. No, I didn't say it was your fault, but did I say how grateful I am that you owe me money so I can experience my own form of wanting to be paid back and then question that and get in touch with my gratitude? Life is a teacher. Money is a teacher. Giving is a teacher. Where's the money? Show me the money? Being grateful has a price.

But thanks for such a good meeting! Wow and more wow. Namaste. It was a great meeting, wasn't it? It was so productive. Even if nothing happened at the meeting it was still a very good meeting because we met. Well not in person but we all tried and that is what counts. Thank you. Now, I know you prefer to call our meeting or rather interaction *an argument*. But the best I can compromise with is calling it a heated verbal exchange especially when I am on my yoga mat. I was wearing my yoga mat panties and I was in a somewhat distressed state for my yoga mat was stolen while I was on it furthering my yoga mat misery. And that you had to call me bitch-whore and then say that I am *the greatest disappointment in your life*. I do hope you stay warm with your infidelity. When I said you were a generous lover I didn't mean with my best friend. Sorry not to clarify but there is always room for improvement!

May I ask, are you praying? Please pray. I did ask my acupuncturist if one could steal private information and betray and still pray. And I am happy to report that it is not a problem at all if you are on your probiotics. Because the gut and the heart are related. Again Grateful! Grateful gut!

Do you have anything to pray for besides a new Tesla for each of your kids and step kids and a personal chef while vacationing in St. Bart's before entering the rehab spa? Nothing has been the same since David Letterman let himself go. He looks like a homeless person. I saw him in St. Bart's and for goodness sake it could have been Greenwich, Connecticut with a tan line.

I wish that Jon Stewart would come back for then everything would be better. How could he leave? I don't know what to watch. There are too many white men on television and I can't decide which one to watch. They all look the same— Jimmy this Jimmy that Jimmy crack corn—but I guess that is my problem.

I should mind my own business but may I take a minute and say I am so lucky to have something to pray for, after I was beaten and I do not remember anything of it. I am so grateful to have something to pray for, even if I do not remember anything of it . . . just a fuzzy wuzzy blur! At least I was able to keep some of my clothing on as you humiliated me. You are so considerate in your jealous rages! At least I won't have to worry about getting a job. I will think only the best of you. Namaste.

Do you know how to give it away? Give it away, all of it? I give it all away before you take it from me. And then I buy it all back. But keep something for yourself. And then give me everything else so I can give it back to you and then I can be generous on your behalf. And then you can be grateful.

I continue to be grateful even when you kick me in the face.

Even when you talk behind my back, at least I am in your thoughts.

I hesitate to tell you my needs so my voice halts to stay the course of centering and staying in the moment. I am grateful. I am generous. I am afraid of you.

Fear provides an opportunity of surrendering serenity dependent on centering no matter how you treat me.

What the fuck are you talking about?

As a woman I know I am not valuable, desirable to you. If you don't want something from my physical looks, I don't exist.

Please don't feel you have to apologize because you hurt my feelings. Oh, my Google no! Ever since I have accepted Google as my god things are so much easier to search! Let go and let Google. Easy Google it! One Google at a time! Keep it Google!

I know that my presence puts you into a state of turmoil and agitation and for that I am indeed sorry. I have tried to be as little trouble as possible even with the affairs. I have tried to think about you, our family. Even though you dropped me off in the middle of nowhere without food or water and to fend for myself I tried to understand your need for closure. Giving me a phone number when I do not have a phone is something I will have to deal with and that is my problem. I tried to not to be too sensitive even though you took me to a steak house when I am a vegetarian. And then when you became vegetarian my weight became more of a talking point. I will not be aggressive even though I was left alone. I will still be grateful for the opportunity to consider the future possibilities of creating a more sustainable relationship that even if it's not possible it could be possible and for that I am very grateful. I

will stay open. And I will run for president. And even when
I lose I will still stay strong. And even when I stand next to you
I will be grateful for the opportunity to lose.

For I stayed open even when you fucked the hell out of
Gennifer, Paula, Kathleen, *what the fuck others who look like*
skunks like his mother and the cigar fuck blue dress scum cum . . .
I am so grateful that I was able to show my resilience and to
try despite your disapproval, and losing the electoral college,
but I won with the popular vote, still I put myself in your
imagination into the oval office into the scene of the action.
But hey it is all worth it for a little bit of power, and you have
to say that through it all at least I finally had a great hair day!
It is all about forgiveness and I am the best at forgiving—
no one can forgive like I forgive—even when the now-
president hovered, stalked my body to show his frame against
my silhouette at the debate. That is why I showed up at the
inauguration for I can love more than the hate of the orange
body. I love my country but I love the opportunity to be the
power at the bottom in order to get to the power at the top.

What the fuck are you talking about?

I am talking about a positive attitude at all costs. I can keep
it together! A country is invaded. A home is invaded. A school

is invaded. A dance club is invaded. A cinema is invaded.
An airport is invaded. A temple is invaded. A studio is invaded.
A body invaded. A brown and black body is invaded.

I struggled with the dread and desperation of the future as
it approaches. And now I no longer have to. Because I lost.
Sometimes you win by losing. I can go back to Chappaqua.
Back to my whiteness luxury. I will be found walking my
dog. I will be berated for debriefing. I will not be allowed to
speak about my experience.

When you do not speak to me I will not see it as being
excluded but rather marvel at your confidence in moving
away from me. When you slip on the ice and hurt your
shoulder, don't despair, you have another shoulder. I have a
shoulder. Or better yet, get off the damn ice.

Would you please just shut the fuck up is not an option to
consider. The most popular female is a victim. We love a
female in trouble. Couldn't someone just rape me? Someone
rape me. Can someone please just rape me for the humiliation
is not working! Nevertheless, I persevere even when I worked
so hard at trying to be accepted, talented. It was never
enough and I forgot that there is always room for another
corrupt white man and well, you know the rest . . .

Because we see ourselves in her in me. Do we prefer a woman down on her luck rather than a woman in charge? We don't like Hillary. I don't like the way she talks. I don't like Hillary for I am Hillary. Even Oprah said you don't have to like Hillary to vote for her. Hey, that's a great show of support! There is just something about her. There is something about me. I can't put my finger on it. Please someone put your finger on it.

But Melania isn't like that. Melania doesn't have to lie or say things she doesn't mean. She doesn't even have to use her own words. She uses Michelle's words.

I identify with my blonde tangled pussy. That is why god counts on cunt.

I asked my yogi then my psychic then my acupuncturist then my accountant then my masseuse then my personal shopper then my aromatherapist why god made Hillary. Why did god make me? Why are you asking me that? There is just something about her. Hillary speaks up and out in a way that makes me uncomfortable. I just can't get anything right!

You know why I don't like her? I don't like a pantsuit! It never fucking worked. These solid color olive green pantsuits . . . couldn't she do paisley or something more Stella McCartney, Marc Jacobs, vintage Willi Smith, Alexander

McQueen, or Pucci? Can't you show your ass, show a panty line! Do some retro Bob Fosse. Give me a sequin, some flashy faux and trim.

But oh god oh god oh god no no no no no—
Thank God we don't have four years of Eileen Fisher!

I want a woman that I can lay my heavy head on
I want a woman that I don't need to think about, only to
    ridicule
See, it is all my fault
I am to blame for everything
Yes, you are
Look into blue
I thought I would be able to heal, forget with power, and
    return to the Oval Office
To do the best job for my country. I love my cuntry.

THE BLUE DRESS

But do you remember the blue dress?
Millennials, do you remember the blue dress of
    Monica Lewinsky?
Google it.
You remember Monica, the White House intern who had
    an affair with President Clinton?
She kept the blue dress she was wearing with Bill's semen.
Monica kept it.
And the FBI subpoenaed Lewinsky for the dress to test the
    DNA during the Clinton impeachment hearing.

Let's think about that blue dress now . . .

Put on the blue dress
Keep on the blue dress
Oh blueness oh blue
Oh, Democratic convention
Shrouded in blue captivity
Takes us back to the earlier infamous cobalt dress
Not the one worn by Michelle at the convention
Not Melania's suit at the inauguration
But an earlier time, in 1997
When twenty-three-year-old Monica Lewinsky
Kept the blue dress with President Clinton's semen
Monica kept it.

Oh, blueness dress
Not greenness nor red nor pink
But navy
Oh, dark sky of night
Or clear sky of day
Oh, midnight mystery
Like waiting for a vanished flight
Lost in oblivion orgasm
The staged sapphire ball
The bluest sky
The coldest hand
The depths of atmosphere tingled skin
Hello blue dress
A delphinium bell skirt
Monica oh Monica let me touch your warmth
Take me to indigo, dear
Don't despair
There are fireworks tonight
Deep blue cerulean
A cadmium, cobalt, or cyan
To come on
Fly into azure and shoot into mid air
My melancholic baby a deep blue sea-ness
With meringue topping

Close enough to hear the melody
Of Delta Blues and Muddy Waters
Oh, democratic blueberries with cream
Turn her tussled dark curls
Into a Blue Serenade a Blue Danube
A Picasso guitar player
Or a glimpse of the Blue Rider
Of frequent guests of the table cloth
To wipe my mouth
And get off
Bring me off, friend
Bring me off, intern
Get me off, girl
Get me off, intern
Take this beast of power
Take this Unicorn horn
Find me the dress–find it now–saved and wrapped
Save the evidence
With a seed bed fitting of a president
Yves Klein blue
His messy hubris spills over
And if you listen you will hear Bill Evans and Miles Davis
A Kind of Blue, and Joni
This blue willow weeps

Let me channel it into a sex relief
It is time to find the clouds in the heavens
Let the winds blow through these royal skies

Oh, little death
Let me fade to blue
And stop the shame of my humble body shake
Frenzy
Hold me hold me intern
Hold this president in your hand
Hold me close
Hold me hard
Oh true blue
Trusted blue steel blue
Blue

For it reminds me: I once said that I did it because I could. But I wasn't lying when I said I never had sexual relations with that woman, that intern. That was my way of having sexual relations with my wife. It was a deeper desperation and with a much bigger satisfaction. Let me come all over this liberty, this truth, the space behind the stars. Let me come all over the blue uniform. I pleasure myself in my primal libido and the charm is when I ask Hillary for forgiveness. There is nothing like it—to see her anger, her support, to see her love without conditions, to see her conditional love. How much can

she put up with? Let her live with my aging body, my inappropriate
advances. How much can she put up with? The sexual tension is in
the strategies of cruelty and running interference.

I couldn't wait to win to see our shared bedroom, the Oval
Office that I would have won. It would be my room now.
And I would grasp Bill's face as he reminisced.
You remember that chair, that phone, our double bed?
I would have touched that phone, the desk—
Where his cock was stroked, fondled, as he listened to
    world leaders on the line.
Bill walks with his blue balls in hand
And recalls a time when he shook the hand of Kennedy
You ruined everything
You ruined everything
Who's wearing the blue dress now?
I'm wearing the blue dress now
Wearing the blue dress
Take off the blue dress
Take off the blue
The blue
Leave it on let me come all over you
Blue
Blue blue blue

Oh depression, oh blueness
Oh sadness, oh sorrow
I'm coming
I'm coming
Coming
Jesus
Jesus
Fuck
Fuck
Oh god
Oh god
Oh goddess
There is still that damn glass ceiling and there is nothing
    but blue

Every day is a little death a little closer to the final day
The final place we work towards and avoid
I am so grateful for today
So grateful.

A ROSE IS A ROSE

You want a job, young thing?
Let me embrace you
I'm a touchie-feelie guy
Stripped naked
A groping lecherous blitz.

Here is your job description:
Accept vulgar phone calls
Panting late at night
Parading naked in your sight
With my ding-dong out,
my journalistic dickhead
I do give a good interview
Shake that ass, I am on PBS!
I will provide coffee-mug bling
And take you on the round oak table.

Yes, be afraid of my Peabody Award power
Over your Little Miss Nobody career
See my explosive tantrums
You want the job?
This is the job:
Let me put my hand on your waxed leg

And sometimes on your upper thigh
Something like the Upper East thigh
I am moving on up!
This is my job search:
Watch me, Ingenue,
As I emerge from the shower
You've heard of the power lunch?
Well, honey, get out the loofah
This is the Power Shower News Hour
An intriguing newsworthy substance
Star-kissed naked Charlie looking for tuna
Ready to hold on to sass at a staff party
That's me,
I got your ass.

Unwanted sexual advances as critical research
At my private waterfront estate
Yeah, I forced myself on you
But, hey, what a view! And ocean air!
While traveling with me in cars
Or in a hotel suite or private plane
Hey, traveling makes me horny
What do ya say?
Want a Mimosa?

I repeatedly call the young thing late at night
Or early in the morning, to get a rise
Express in detail my fantasy starring Mademoiselle
Swimming naked in my pool
As I gaze from my master suite
Sweet
That's just Charlie being Charlie

Oh, come on, what's wrong with
An unwanted shoulder grab
Call me crusty lusty grandpaw claw
Unleashed bathrobe, dog unchained
Wagging underneath
Dog is out of the yard
This doggy bites
The new girl shoves his tail away
and weeps.

Throughout the attack
The assault
The hazing of young women being beckoned
The Hamptons is so stylishly reckoned
Permit entry, ajar not so far

Turn on hot shower pressure
I call her name, *insistently*
for my working pleasure
Ignoring him, she is there to work
Boss leaves the shower and stands over her
She turns her head, she has a brain
See my skin
Drop the towel
Don't you avoid the sight!
Didn't you hear me call you?
Something to look forward to in the future
A male coworker, cackling says
Oh, you got the shower dick, I mean trick
LOL

"One of the most important and influential people in
    journalism"
If this is the best then God help me from the worst
Maybe I can work myself up to Harvey
I have so much to look forward to

I liked grabbing you by the hair
I had a hard day
Public television can be such a bitch

I know I was yelling at you, calling you stupid incompetent
    pathetic
But I paid your expenses
I tried to be considerate as I molested you as you wept
Baby, oh baby, why are you crying?
I was hunting for a job, she sobbed
No, baby, you got it wrong
I am hunting you.

PUSSY SPEAK OUT

Men, pay attention
When we say No
We mean No
Do not push your body on any of us
Rape, violations, assaults
Hotel sex crimes
Hidden kept secret harassment
Assault disguised as job interview
30 years of abuse?
Try 3,000 years
Over 90 accusations with just one Harvey
Every woman doesn't expect this to happen in her lifetime
but it happens to every single woman
Repeatedly
Guaranteed
Intergenerationally
Spoken between women
Mothers to daughters to granddaughters
Amongst friends
We are taught how to use your body at times
To feign interest till you get to safety, a pause in his release
How to disembody, dissociate as you are raped
Taught to forget yet remember and hold the pain and fear
the shame

Hating your body
yet the desire is abjection
Held as object
Trained and groomed

Grab 'em by the pussy
A president's war cry
Whether Bill or some other friendly neoliberal
Or some conservative cock
It is like eating a chicken sandwich
Take-out
Power of pussy

Harvey Handlers & Enablers:
To keep your jobs
Enforcing silence
For another slobbering box of popcorn
For some other film
Probably made and directed by a man
Where man gets girl

Turning down the sheets
To get to the script
Appearing naked

Coaxing young women
To overpower intimate
grabbed encounters

Massage explicit messages
with oil and motion
It never stops with a backrub
Keep me safe
manipulationfearingretaliationembarrassmentpainrapesob
bingdistraught*locked*inavanaroomajobadeskanoffice,
A car, get the pillow to his room, bathroom disturbed
angry take me out of here let me go no no no no
passing out here you are here help me
I

Together we stand
Band together in solidarity
Women unite
Oh, hello young beauty
Here is your predator
One powerful male producer
Known as the Hollywood system
A systemic industry thin and full of botox
and cleavage

To force his hairy self
You are perfect for the upcoming role
as rag doll for Harvey
No one stopped him
No one from the company
No one from the board
Never stopped
Too much money
To be made
Not too bad
Put up with it
Sign a Nondisclosure clause
While he's giving money to a liberal cause.

Mr. Weinstein, known for outbursts tirades explosions
Private and public pounding
But it was the particular female
that he enjoyed the most
and gave of his most personal self
Hurting the most vulnerable young woman
a female who wanted, who had ambition
Who desired to work, had talent
He was brutal in shaming and punishing this woman
for her desire to be an actress, to work in the field

Written off as just another form of toxicity
Coercive bargaining to keep quiet and maybe a chance
    at a script
For the hopeful actress, meeting with the god as devil
Might generate a deal, an opportunity, a chance
to be part of what you had trained for
but first you had to do Harvey
penetrated, sucked, licked, or eaten
It was never your choice

The pain is so bad
to keep your soul from slipping
as you clutch to whatever dream you
can salvage in this
nightmare
As he enters as you cry out
Harvey ejaculates
feeling her fear that then transforms his power to prove he
    is a man
He is in charge and takes her power
He has the plan:
I will force myself
Eat you and you eat me

For it is a dog eat dog world
I am so ugly—so ugly but you will eat this ugly.

Ram it down your throat, you won't have anything like me.
There is no way out. There is only a way in. I despise women.
I hate women for I want them and I am so ugly that I can
only force myself on them for fear of rejection. They only
want one thing. They are actress whores.
And all of this to make a *moving* image
Where we can all sit in the darkened theater
together in the dark
Left alone
Survivors
Left in the dark
That's entertainment!

It is not just the ravishing actress
On stage or screen
For it is in all walks of life and career
A woman poses a risk to herself
Her body is dangerous
A potential target of attack
She presents by her presence

At all times, everywhere and anywhere
The male has the dominion to punish and beat and violate
A passionate uncontrollable rage
Her body pushes him to the edge
He is built that way
He can't help himself
That is how men are

We know your life your body has value, Women
You speak truth
You aren't lying
You aren't bringing this on
You didn't dress this way
You weren't expecting this
Wherever you work and live
Whatever you do
Whoever you are
Women unite we won't stand and be raped, groped, abused,
    mocked, and violated.
Women girls females identified trans people
deserve to be treated with dignity
Your body is yours
Respect our body
This body is mine

It is not here for you
The time has come for female empowerment
We won't be ridiculed and our bodies occupied for your
   benefit
No more codes of silence
No more silence
Pussy speak out.

UNICORN GRATITUDE

While some folks are feeling fucked over these days—in particular, white liberals—black, brown, and marginalized, othered bodies have endured US policy since the first Thanksgiving.

AFTERMATH

When my liberal mood is upset
I just can't take the news, the media, climate change
Like a day when there is a tragedy
or something upsetting
Your candidate's email is being hacked
Or the election is rigged
Or your pussy is grabbed
Or that a wall is being built
Or the farmer's market is out of frisée!
Endive will not do
Radicchio will not do
Sorrel will not do
Fiddleheads will not do.
What do you mean the farmer's market is out of frisée and
    champagne vinegar?
What do you mean freeze dried mango is out of stock?
The world is falling apart and I was planning on having
    frisée this weekend!
EVERYTHING GREEN IS AGAINST ME

What kind of farmer's market is this?

No baby arugula or baby kale?

Did you hear me and do you know who I am?

For goddess sake—is this or isn't this Silicon Valley,
Union Square, Westchester, Marina del Rey, or the
North Shore?

I want free range and grass fed

I want broccoli slaw and chia sprouts

I am ready for a scene

My breakfast flax seeds are going to spill

I want homegrown and local farm to table. I want a
multi-cultural ankle bracelet at a discount. This can't
be happening.

I buy fair trade, sustainable and artisanal

This can't be happening to me!

*The way to stay focused is to close your eyes and think of jewel
tones on a pant suit. Imagine the colors of sapphires, emeralds,
rubies, topaz, pink diamonds, garnets. Move to fire opals and pearls,
semi-precious stones. Amethysts, turquoise, amber and aquamarine,
carnelian, coral, jade and jasper, lapis lazuli, moonstone, onyx,
peridot, rose quartz, tiger's eye and bloodstone, tourmaline and
zircon. Engage the term precious. Ah, all better now. Precious. You
are so precious to me.*

Can we all stop?
Let us take a moment
Just stop and imagine together . . . the Unicorn
A Unicorn collective consciousness
A Unicorn collective unconsciousness
Oh, I love a Unicorn
Who doesn't love a Unicorn?
I love a Unicorn on a backpack or a fanny pack
It reveals mystical mythical enchantment
The white-horned creature alone
With a rainbow world to adore
The white Unicorn encircles my throat as a choker
With iron-on glitter for an all-cotton t-shirt
It is the illusion, the magical kingdom within
Of enchanted whiteness and purity without
Imagined mythical extinct being in pure white
Neoliberal creature

The Unicorn is here
The Unicorn is here
The Unicorn is there
Hello Unicorn
The Unicorn has a golden halo with rainbow curls

The Unicorn has a reality show and has no lines to memorize
The Unicorn never wears a mask
The Unicorn always has grass under its feet and is loyal
The Unicorn is a great communicator and still enjoys
    silence
    and pauses
(pause)
(silence)

The Unicorn understands cinema
The Unicorn and the moon are one
A Unicorn moon
The Unicorn has passion for a mystery that does not
    yet exist
There is no job too small for the Unicorn
Even without hands the Unicorn will get the job done
The relationship with the Unicorn is always superficial
But not in a superficial way
The Unicorn does not believe in analysis (but in tapestry)
The Unicorn's standards are always evolving
The Unicorn is hope and wishes
The Unicorn has empathy for difference and imagination,
    within reason
The Unicorn prefers the dragon roll to the California roll

But will think twice about the spider roll

Oh, Unicorn let us continue to sing your praise!

The Unicorn can calmly explain the meaning of lyrical, repeatedly

The Unicorn does not like Styrofoam under any circumstances

The Unicorn does not like to think too far ahead

But does like something to look forward to (involving pesto and ramps)

The Unicorn doesn't mind being called Uni-Porn

The Unicorn has plans for an umbrella empire with a virtual presence on Amazon Prime

The Unicorn likes Pellegrino with no ice

Since the Unicorn doesn't exist they never need to worry about identity theft, deleted emails or the G train

 Or anything, for that matter

URL really stands for Unicorn Reality Longitude

Is the Unicorn angry? That is the question

The beauty of the Unicorn is when you are wasted you never waste your time with the Unicorn.

In other words, time is never wasted with the Unicorn

The Unicorn starts with you (U) so you are the Unicorn

Let's have a Unicorn revolution

The Unicorn returned to Vermont

The Unicorn attended Montessori

The Unicorn appreciates cake

The Unicorn banished aluminum and Teflon

The Unicorn never apologizes on a full stomach

The Unicorn prefers to travel alone

The Unicorn is a state of mind rather than a state of being

The Unicorn can appear at any time

The Unicorn likes its kale massaged *please*

The Unicorn likes its horn massaged with almond oil
    please

Captivity, a couch, Kumbucha, and small batch cider with a
    griffin insignia is the end to the Unicorn universe as we
    know it

The Unicorn does not push buttons

The Unicorn will not be put on hold

The Unicorn turns it horn when the blizzard of '67 is
    brought up

The Unicorn once met Studs Terkel

The Unicorn volunteers for something with pineapples
    and sparkles

The Unicorn reports to a Jungian analyst about a dream of
    the Chicago Seven taking turns riding on its back

The Unicorn loved the salad bars in the 80s and into the
    90s, and never looked back

The Unicorn makes its own wind chimes

The Unicorn has student debt and lives in up and coming gentrified neighborhoods on Thursdays and in already gentrified neighborhoods on alternate weekends

The Unicorn doesn't give a shit and would love to make a rainbow poopy in a field or sports bar

The Unicorn regrets never going mainstream and prime time

The Unicorn embellishes how they suffer to make better art

The Unicorn's 53% of female white women relatives make Unicorn slime

but still voted for Trump

The Unicorn likes the profit margin

The Unicorn bought good shoes to march

The Unicorn took selfies with a pink hat and then went back to binge-watching *The Crown*

The Unicorn has met Eileen Myles

The Unicorn does not like to count money

Net worth makes the Unicorn invisible except when they are wearing linen and eating nasturtiums

Imagine the Unicorn

All is possible with the Unicorn

Replace fear with the Unicorn

Replace anxiety with the Unicorn

We are grateful for the Unicorn
Unicorn, you are so precious to me.

Shut the fuck up, Unicorn!
I am so tired of imagination
I am so tired of hearing about your fucking needlepoint
    portraits at The Met and The Cloisters, of the
    possibilities for inspiration
Was the Unicorn there to save the lion? The giraffe?
Was the Unicorn there for Sandra Bland?
Where were you, Unicorn, for the those in the church
    in Charleston?
When will you show up, Unicorn, in the Windy City?
Where were you, Unicorn, as Trayvon opened the
    rainbow skittle?
Where were you, horned creature, when Eric Garner
    gasped for air?
Where was your magic for Philando Castille?
Take your white lies and your medieval terror liberal
    enchantment bullshit
Hell to you, you white savior beast
Damn your white preciousness and impossible chivalry that
    I am part of

I won't sit still for you to appear with magical enchantment

There is no Unicorn for me

There is no Unicorn for you

There is no Unicorn for me

There is no Unicorn for you

There is no Unicorn for us

Three white-horn rhinos are all that are left.

SPECIAL ACKNOWLEDGMENTS

This book would not be possible if not for the support of so many in my life. A heartfelt thank you to my brilliant editor, the one and only Amy Scholder, who I have had the honor and pleasure to collaborate with on many book projects. Her literary talent, friendship, and perspective is treasured by me and has been instrumental in the text's vision. But all of this would not happen at all without the inspiration, guidance, and leadership of Colin Robinson with OR Books. Thank you Colin for your dedication, courage, and enthusiasm for championing writing as activism for social change. It is a privilege to have the opportunity to work with you, John Oakes, and the wonderful staff at OR Books. Thank you Emma Ingrisani for your skills in managing the production, and Elyse Strongin for design.

I would like to acknowledge the provenance of the writing. *This Land is Not Their Land* and *Trump Said* was first performed at the Montalvo Art Center as an artist-in-residence for a project with Bruce Yonemoto. These texts were also included as part of the film directed by Bruce Yonemoto, *Far East of Eden,* commissioned by Montalvo Art Center. I would like to thank the Sally and Don Lucas Artists Residency Program and the Montalvo Art Center, staff and board for their support. Thank you Bruce Yonemoto, Bryan Jackson, Kelly Sicat, Angela McConnell, T. M. Ravi, and the board of Montalvo for their support. Thank you Bruce for your friendship and collaboration. The film was screened at Museum of Modern Art NYC, curated by Kathy Brew.

Some of the text from the performance *Unicorn Gratitude Mystery* is included in the book which was first produced by Spin Cycle in NYC at Laurie Beechman Theater. Thank you Chip Duckett and Ron Lasko for your continued support. And to Violet Overn for production, dramaturgy, costume, and video design for *Unicorn*. And to Casey Wyman for video art. It has also been produced at Steppenwolf, Chicago; Hallwalls, Buffalo, NY; LaMama, NYC; REDCAT theater, Los Angeles; La Pietra NYU, Florence, as part of the Women and Migration conference; Museum of Art and Design, Miami; and VFD, London. My deep appreciation goes to Greta Honold, Ed Cardoni, Nicky Paraiso, Mark Murphy, Deb Willis, Ellyn Toscano, Sebastián Calderón Bentin, Uli Baer, Rina Carvajal, Phoebe Patey-Ferguson, Lyall Hakaraia. Thank you to all of the people involved for supporting the development and producing the work.

I would like to acknowledge all of the support from my many inspiring colleagues, students, and administrators at NYU, and the department of Art and Public Policy at Tisch School of the Arts. I am so appreciative to be able to work, learn, and teach here.

Thank you to my family and friends. I am so blessed to have such wonderful people in my life. To all the Finleys and a special thanks to Brian Finley, Marline Johnson, Michael Overn, Cathy O'Connor, Dona Ann McAdams, Nancy Howard Gray, Lori E. Seid, Becky Hubbert, Johanna Went, Chris Tanner, Mat Gleason, Adonis Volanakis, Marsea Goldberg, David Roman, Ricardo Gamboa, Andy Somma, Joanne Telser-Frere, Nan Becker, Mary D. Dorman, Christopher Audain, Joseph Varisco, Offer Egozy, and John Sims. And finally, to Violet Overn, my precious daughter who inspires me with her activism, feminism and creativity.

Photo by Timothy Greenfield-Sanders

KAREN FINLEY is an artist and writer whose work has long provoked controversy and debate. She has performed at Lincoln Center (NYC), the Barbican Centre (London), Steppenwolf (Chicago), and the Bobino (Paris). Her art is in the collection of the Centre Pompidou in Paris and the Museum of Contemporary Art in Los Angeles, among other places. She has received numerous awards, including a Guggenheim Fellowship, two Obies, two Bessies, and a *Ms.* magazine Woman of the Year Award. Her previous books include *Shock Treatment*, *Enough is Enough*, *Living It Up*, *A Different Kind Of Intimacy*, *George & Martha*, and *The Reality Shows*. Finley is a professor in the Department of Art and Public Policy at Tisch School of the Arts, New York University.